LIFE
IN THE
PALACE

LIVING A SPIRIT-FILLED LIFE

Life in the Palace

Living a Spirit-filled Life

Dr. David Donnally

© 2022 David Donnally

All rights reserved

ISBN 978-1-7353828-5-2

No part of this book may be reproduced, stored in a retrieval system, or transmitted in any form or by any means, electronic, mechanical, photocopying, recording or otherwise without the written permission of the author.

Emerge Publishing Group, LLC

Riviera Beach, Fl

561-601-0349

Dr. David Donnally 2022

Life in the Palace

Printed in the United States of America

Dedication:

Thanks first to God Almighty, my King.

I would also like to thank my loving wife, who without her support this book could not have happened. And to my beautiful daughter Victoria, son-in-law Billy, and my grandchildren Billy IV and Nevaeh, and the generations to come.

I pray that Kingdom living will always be your desire.

I thank my loving parents who enjoyed abundant life in part, but now enjoy abundant life in whole.

And to my dear friends, Gary and Susan Richard, who have taught me the true meaning of friendship.

Table Of Contents

Preface...	7
Chapter #1 – Love	9
Chapter #2 – Joy...	21
Chapter #3 – Peace...	27
Chapter #4 – Longsuffering..................................	35
Chapter #5 – Kindness...	39
Chapter #6 – Goodness..	43
Chapter #7 – Faithfulness.....................................	47
Chapter #8 – Gentleness..	53
Chapter #9 – Self Control.....................................	57
Chapter #10 – Protection......................................	75
Chapter #11 – Victory...	89
Chapter #12 – Our God Reigns............................	95
Conclusion...	111
About the Author..	113

Preface

Life in the Palace will help the believer to have a good basic understanding of what the Spirit-filled life should look like. When Jesus came and gave His life, he didn't just pay for our sins. He made it possible for believers to be cleansed so His precious Holy Spirit could come and dwell within us.

Before Jesus (in the old covenants), this indwelling was to be only temporary. But now, because of His blood sacrifice, we are washed and cleansed. His Spirit can once again dwell in us. We can now be redeemed, renewed, and restored to the original format of relationship.

For as in Adam, all die—every environment. Even so, in Christ shall all be made alive (new, whole, restored). Some may think this can never happen until death, but, if this were true, then when we accept Christ, we would die immediately and go to Heaven. Jesus came to save that which was lost. Abundant living can start today! I pray as you read this book you will be encouraged to move into Palace Living today!

Chapter 1

> *And now these three remain: faith, hope and love. But the greatest of these is love.*
>
> I Corinthians 13:13

KEY #1 "LOVE"

LOVE IS THE FIRST KEY TO PALACE LIFE.

Love is the key to relationships. So, where does this love come from?

As in my first book, *From the Pond to the Palace*, I start where all abundant living starts and that is with love. Love in the kingdom is all around. Love from other citizens in the kingdom, love from those whom you have helped find the Palace, love from the leaders to the people and from the people to the leaders, love for the King and the King's love of his people, love for the rules that keep the kingdom safe and healthy, and yes, even love for those still outside the Kingdom—still living in the pond.

Now there will be those outside the kingdom, non-believers in our King and all he stands for and they may even hate us. Maybe because they don't understand, or we have not shown the proper love for them. In either case we must try to always show the King's love for all.

Never forget the King's Word says that we are blessed when others hate us for the King's sake. We should never feel bad, but be joyful when others hate and revile us for our relationship with the King, or our position as a Palace Dweller.

Love is not always the easiest road, and some are harder to love than others. I have found in my many years of ministry that some people have not known love, so it is almost impossible for them to love others. Some can't, some won't, but most of us want to love and be loved! We must always remember that love is a decision. We must decide to love.

We learn how to love when we experience the true love of the King, and his people begin to be healed of hurt, pain or circumstances that caused or continue to cause us not to love or to let others love us. Sometimes when husbands can't love their wives and when love is absent from the marriage, the wife may feel neglected, and the children may not see what a loving couple should look like. So how will they ever be able to love? Sometimes we just don't like people. They turn us off by things they do or say, and these feelings can keep us from being able to love.

In the Kingdom we learn that the King was worthy to lay down all that he had (<u>all</u>), even His very life. It is by His stripes that we are healed. There is no greater love than this—to be willing to lay down one's life for others.

When we accept the King's invitation to come into the Kingdom and live in His presence we will love others, love ourselves and love Him who first loved us.

Now this doesn't mean that in the Kingdom we will never be upset with other citizens, but when we focus on the King and what He has done for us and others we will remember we have freely received His love so we should freely give His love. Love is the glue that makes the body one.

You can't love someone with the love of the King and hate them at the same time. In the Kingdom there is abundant, amazing love. There is a song that says, "Amazing love how can it be that you my King would die for me."

When we focus on the King and his amazing love we can love more effectively. Husbands realize they are to love their wives as Christ loves the church and gave His life for it. Wives should love their husbands and submit to his authority as unto the Lord. Children should honor and love their parents that their days will be long. Parents should love their children and train them in the way they should go.

We should love our neighbor as ourselves and the Lord our God and King with all of our heart, soul, mind, and strength. Yes! Love is abundant in the Kingdom. And it is ours. *Life in the Palace* begins with LOVE.

LOVE IS RIGHTNESS - RIGHT AND PERFECT

Love is right, love is kind. Love in the kingdom brings right living and righteousness. The King's law says there is none righteous no, not one. But that is without the King. For in the kingdom under his command, and because of his sacrifice, we become righteous. Not because of who we are or what we have done, but because of who He is (the King) and what He has done (redeemed us and washed us whiter than snow), we become right.

Now what is right? Our society, the world view tells us right is relative. One man's patriot is another man's terrorist. Right seems to be whatever spin someone puts on an action. But the Word is what the King says, there is a way that seems right unto a man. It is broad and easy but leads to destruction. Our King says straight is the path and narrow the gate that leads to righteousness, or not so easy. So how would we ever be able to take this hard road or path to righteous Palace living? Only through and with the King. Remember we are together, not alone. He loves us and is always with us. We can and do live righteously because we are with Him and He is with us. We are perfected because of Him, we are righteous because of Him.

Love Brings Light

Because we are with Him and He is with us, His love shines through us as a beacon to a lost and darkened world. The more we love the brighter we shine. The brighter we shine the more others who are still in darkness, can see the Kingdom as a bright city of hope.

When someone first walks into a dark room, they usually say, "Give me a minute so my eyes can adjust to the darkness." We in the church unfortunately have let our eyes get adjusted to the darkness and we don't recognize how limited our vision has become.

We must remove the scales and take off the blinders and begin to love with the love of the King so we can shine brightly once more.

Now remember we are not the light. The love of God in us (the Holy Spirit) is the light. We simply reflect light like the moon reflects the sun or clean mirror reflects the light.

In the Kingdom, the love of the King is reflected in the eyes, heart, and lives of His people (the citizens of the Kingdom). Others can see the King's love through our reflection. We must do our best to keep our mirrors clean from debris that may dim that light. Love shines brightest when the vessels are clean. We can bring hope, light, and life to a lost world if we just love God our King and let His love shine through us.

LOVE IS PURE – NOT PERVERTED

In the age that we live much is said about love that really isn't true. Some have said love stinks, love hurts, love kills, love starts wars, etc. But true pure love does none of these, for God is love.

Let's look at the one aspect of love people like to pick on the most: Love of our King causes us to want to destroy or kill those of other kingdoms. This is not true. Our King is the one and only king. So, you are either in the Kingdom or out. He says in his laws He wants all to be part of the Kingdom, but if we don't want to, we don't have to; but we cannot share all the benefits if we do not take on the responsibility of Kingdom living. We must love everyone. Yes, everyone! Man has always done things in the name of religion but when you become part of the Kingdom of God you see a lot more clearly. You recognize religion is not the same as love.

Another form of love being perverted is euthanasia—the taking of one's life in the name of love. This is a topic many writers will stay away from because of political correctness, but this is not a book on politics; it is on Kingdom living. Loving someone and watching them suffer is a very hard thing. But in the Kingdom, we have the King's decree that says the King gives and the King taketh away; Blessed be the name of the King. Simply put, life and death are in His hands, not ours.

Keeping someone alive by artificial means when they have an irreversible prognosis, and then deciding to remove life support at this point is not euthanasia. Euthanasia (happy death) is when we or someone we love is going through a tough terminal illness. To eliminate the downward cycle and possible suffering of them and family, that person decides that they should make the death decision, themselves, and end their life. Even though they or family may think this is for the best, they have taken the responsibility away from the King and said they know best—not Him who made them.

When someone is so weak that they can't eat, and you allow for a natural death this does not show a lack of love; this is not euthanasia. Refusing treatment for a terminal illness is not euthanasia. This in no way stops or hinders the King from healing you or taking you to be with Him. Many pervert the name of love by acts of passion, but our King teaches us from Corinthians chapter 13:4-13 we learn what is true love:

> *Love suffereth long and is kind.*
>
> *Love envies not.*

Love vaunteth not itself.

Love is not puffed up.

Love does not behave unseemly.

Love seeketh is not her own.

Love is not easily provoked.

Love thinketh no evil.

Love rejoices not in iniquity.

Love rejoices in the truth.

Love believeth all things.

Love beartheth all things.

Love hopeth all things.

Love endureth all things.

Love never fails.

Now abides faith, hope, love, but the greatest of these is love.

Yes, some may try to pervert love, but the King's law tells us what love truly is. And when we truly start living in the Kingdom, we realize there will come a day when this world passes away and we are in that city where the SON always shines. The love we have now will be with us then. We will no longer need hope, for we will be where we hoped for. We will no longer have faith for it has become sight—but love shall still be ours now and then and forever. Praise God. Life in the Palace is love. Amen

LOVE AND MARRIAGE

Many times, people have come to me asking that age old question, "Should I marry, or do you think he or she is the right one?" My answer to them is formed in the question, "Does the King say you should marry?" Not mom or dad or pastor or talk show host or doctor or whoever, but the King. To be able to know what the King wants for you, you must know Him and the way to know Him is to know His Word. In the previous chapter reference was made to I Corinthians 13 (The love chapter). When we find out what love is all about or that love is all about the King, we see more clearly who that person will be, and we can share Palace living with someone here on earth. We recognize that there will be no marriage in Heaven when we look to the marriage vow "till death do us part." But let's get back to this temporal plan.

Many will say if it is so simple why do one in every two Christian marriages end in divorce? Just about the same percentage as non-Christians. However, when you have some other questions like do you and your spouse attend and/or are involved in church? Do you pray and have devotions together? Do you live Kingdom life? Do you practice stewardship? Do you follow Kingdom principles in your marriage? When couples do these things, they thrive, and the marriage will last. Kingdom living will dramatically change that percentage. The family that *prays* together *stays* together. Married palace dwellers following Kingdom principles *stay* together.

Here are three things which attack marriage and couples:
1. Satan: he does not want the family to stand, for it is the structure that God ordained so he wants to destroy it.
2. Insensitivity: not thinking of the other but ourselves only. Couples should always try to bring joy to each other. When we have joy, we have peace. Love is joyfully caring about another.
3. Negativity: negative words, actions, or feelings can destroy people from the inside out. The power of positive words and actions can motivate and inspire, build up instead of tear down. In a loving relationship we should try to speak words that bring about a positive response. Now speaking the truth in love can sometimes be taken negatively, so we must always temper our speech with love actions. If we truly love someone you must tell the truth in love with love.

Yes, sin will destroy. For the wages of sin is death but the gift of God our King, is eternal life. The King offers us life, a more abundant life. The Word of God says if you seek first the kingdom of God and his righteousness then all these things (love, marriage, family protection etc.) will be added unto you. So how do we know who to marry, to love etc.? We must trust in the King. Through His precious Holy Spirit, He will guide us into all truth. Love and marriage are not just a commitment but a covenant. Our covenant with each other and His covenant with us. Married life in the palace is wonderful. Does that mean we're happy all the time? No, but we should be speaking about what the Lord has done. Speak positive things about your spouse. Don't air your dirty laundry in public! Marriage teachings could be a separate book, but for our look at palace living, it is abundant living by both spouses that will bless a marriage.

Now, if one spouse lives in the palace and one outside the palace it will be very difficult to make this work. I would say impossible, but as we love in the palace, we learn nothing is impossible with the King. We must be constantly trying to get our spouse to move into the palace.

Never give in, never say never, and don't give in to the feeling that your life on the outside with your spouse would be the same as life together in the palace. Nothing comes close to living in the kingdom with all the King's promises, nothing. So, Kingdom living brings abundantly blessed marriages, and this will bring others to the King.

He chastenth whom he loveth. Discipline is not punishment. Love is disciplining our children.

We know that parents love even when it hurts. Yes, God our King will bring conviction on those even in the Kingdom, but this is because he loves us so much. He desires to guide us through his Holy Spirit into all truth and sometimes this is done with a still small voice and sometimes He allows other things to come to remind us He cares, and he loves enough to discipline. Now, most don't look at discipline as a way to show love, but any parent will tell you it hurts them more and that's the truth. So, if it hurts our King to have to discipline us, why does He do it? Because He loves us too much to let us destroy our chance at Kingdom Living.

So, the next time you feel you may be getting corrected, stop and listen to what the King is saying or as my dad would say to me stop talking and listen, you just might learn something. Well, I did. I learned when I didn't stop and listen, dad would make me stop and listen, so I learned it was much easier on me if I complied. God's Word has much to teach us about Palace Life, but we must listen. Oh, how he loves you and me.

Now, are all tragedies discipline?

Many years ago, hurricanes hit New Orleans. Some said this was God's discipline on the sinful area. God's discipline is His not ours. It is not up to us to say why, what, or who God (the King) is disciplining. It is like seeing a neighbor scolding his son right after their house was on fire and we assume the son started that fire because the dad is scolding him, when the fire started because of faulty wiring, or an electric device and the son had nothing to do with it. The dad was scolding him because his son wanted to run back in to try and save some video games. His dad was telling him it was not worth it to risk his life for material things.

When we see things that we call bad, we must realize some important palace concepts:

1. The King decides. We don't have to worry; He knows the beginning from the end.
2. We are His children; He loves us, and all is for our good.
3. Everything belongs to Him. He can do whatever he wants—it's all His. We are just stewards.
4. He keeps all His promises, for they are all true.
5. God never says whoops! He makes no mistakes.

Love then is the first key to palace living.

Love is the key to all relationships.

Love is righteousness.

Love is not perverted.

Love makes palace marriage blessed.

Love includes discipline.

Chapter 2

The joy of the Lord is my strength.

Nehamiah 8:10

KEY #2 "JOY"

JOYFUL LIFE IS THE KEY TO TRUE HAPPINESS. JOY COMES FROM FREEDOM.

Where there is love there is joy, and true joy comes from the King. He gives us freedom and this freedom gives us the ability to live life. Just as freedom in the United States was bought at a great price with many men and women sacrificing their lives, our Palace Life freedom was bought with a great price. He gave His life for us and shed his blood that we may have life, Palace Life, free life, and yes, abundant life.

Many might think that life in the palace is filled with rules and regulations; however, this is not true. There are only two rules and on the these hang all the rules of Palace Life. First, love the Lord thy God with all our heart soul mind and strength and our neighbor as ourselves. The story of the Good Samaritan in Luke 10 teaches us who our neighbor truly is. Take time to read this story even if you think you know it (Luke 10:25 – 37).

With this freedom comes responsibility. When a teenager first gets his/her license to drive, most parents have a list of responsibilities. The teen soon realizes there is more freedom but also more responsibility. Things like taking time to take care of the car, giving rides to school to younger siblings, maybe paying for car insurance, gas, maintenance etc. So, our life in the United States is filled with freedom but we also have responsibilities, things like voting, taxes, community service, serving and helping others.

Freedom definitely brings joy.

What does Kingdom joy sound like? It sounds like music, singing, dancing, clapping, and rejoicing. What does Kingdom joy look like? The word tells us that the Hebrews rejoiced with singing dancing and music of all types—shofars, trumpets, harps, etc. The Word tells us to make a joyful noise all ye lands, serve the Lord with gladness, come before His presence with singing.

In the Palace you will not only see joy, but you will also hear joy, and you will feel joy. Singing has been part of Christian living and will continue in Palace Living and, I believe, in Heaven living. Music is a medium that transcends where words cannot. Poems and Scripture that are heartfelt or should I say Holy Spirit inspired can touch even the hardest heart.

You know when you hear this type of music because it moves you. It is not just good, fun, nicely arranged or well performed. It comes in power, with power that ministers to our very soul and spirit. His Spirit bears witness with our spirit, we connect.

I have had the privilege of hearing some great music over the years. My dad was a national fiddle champion and had an amazing musical gift. My heart has been stilled many times with a simple melody.

I believe music and rejoicing brings laughter and a light heart and fills the air with sounds, sweet, the sweetest that's ever been heard. Songs like <u>Oh How I love Jesus</u>, <u>We are Standing on Holy Ground</u>, <u>We Exalt Thee</u>, and the list goes on and on and on. Joyful living, Palace Living fills the air with the King's praise. There is no place for the sounds of hatred, bitterness, anger, or strife.

What Does Joyful Living Look Like?

There is a smile on each face. Smiling sometimes looks a little out of place, like at a funeral. But in the Palace, we understand there is a better life to come, no more sickness, no more sadness, no more sorrow. Yes, we can taste what that life will be. Now, some would debate that we can have it now. I think Jesus was telling us we can because He constantly talked about the Kingdom. If it was impossible to live that way here, he would have said *when we die* the Kingdom will be, but He said *this is how we should live*. If He lives in us then where He is, the Kingdom of God is. The Holy Spirit dwells in us.

We have become joint heirs with Jesus. Joyful living looks like royalty, we are part of the family of God! Being part of the King's family makes us all royalty. Joyful living looks like a palace full of princes and princesses, therefore, joyful living is one of purpose and worth. You have a role; you have a value.

So much is said today of kids needing a good self-image. One big reason so many think so little of themselves is they don't know or never been told who they really are in Christ. They are royalty. They are princes and princesses. They have worth not because of who the world tells them they are, but because of who the King says they are. They are the King's children and thus they are heirs to the Kingdom. So, it becomes not who they are, but whose they are. That makes all the difference.

We do not have to make everyone a winner in the game so everyone would feel good about themselves. We could teach them the truth about how competition makes everyone work or train, practice to improve to become the best they can be for the King's glory. So, when we act, we bring pleasure to the King. The King is not impressed with little effort, the King is not impressed with us hiding our talent but using what we have been given to the most and best use possible. Remember the parable of the talents (Matthew 25:14-20).

That parable teaches about those who were given two or five talents. The only one the Lord was displeased with was the one who did not try. The others were blessed. So, this teaches us that effort matters but results matter too. The one who gained the most was blessed with the extra one because he could do the most with it. Now before everyone out there thinks that I'm saying that God is not pleased with those who know how to kick back and relax allowing someone else do all the work, I am saying just that joyful working is a part of Palace Living. You know—the whistle while you work!

We should be joyful in our work for the King. Joyful giving, joyful living, going hand in hand, for the joy of the Lord is our strength. There is an old song that says, *"Are we downhearted, no, no, no troubles may come, and troubles may go. We trust in Jesus, come will or woe."* Are we serving joyfully or halfhearted? We should have a joy filled heart full of God the King's love and blessing.

JOYFUL LIVING IS GOOD FOR OUR HEALTH.

When you feel good you look good and when you feel bad, you look bad. When you are tired and run down or run over you need to remember where your joy comes from. Regain your health by being in the presence of the King.

There are a lot of people who say they have joy but it's hard to see in those broken down, tired, sore, aching bodies. Now our King knows what he is doing and sometimes He will be glorified in our affliction like Paul. At times like this, we must say, "Your grace is sufficient for me." But while common health and wealth are ours in the Palace some of us are satisfied with our conditions. However, remember that the King says, *"Ask and you shall receive that your joy might be full."* Sometimes we have not because we ask not.

WHERE IS JOY?

Men have pursued joy in every avenue imaginable. Some have successfully found it while others have not. Perhaps it would be easier to describe where joy *cannot* be found.

Not in unbelief—Voltaire was an infidel of the most pronounced type. He wrote, "I wish I had never been born."

Not in pleasure—Lord Byron lived a life of pleasure if anyone did. He wrote, "The worm, the canker, and grief are mine alone."

Not in money—Jay Gould, American millionaire, had plenty of that. When dying, he said, "I suppose I am the most miserable man on earth."

Not in position and fame—Lord Beaconsfield enjoyed more than his share of both. He wrote, "Youth is a mistake; manhood a struggle; old age a regret."

Not in glory—Alexander the Great conquered the known world in his day. Having done so he wept in his tent, before saying, "There are no more worlds to conquer."

Where then is real joy found? The answer is simple, in Christ alone.

We have not because we asked not. Have you asked for joyful health? When Jesus healed there was jumping and leaping and praising God. Let's start jumping and leaping and watching what the King does. He loves to see His Palace Dwellers filled with praise and joy filled living. That's what Palace Living is.

Chapter 3

> *You will keep him in perfect peace, whose mind is stayed on you, because he trusts in you.*
>
> Isaiah 26:3

KEY #3 "PEACE"

TRUE PEACE COMES FROM WITHIN.

Long ago a man sought the perfect picture of peace. Not finding one that satisfied, he announced a contest to produce this masterpiece. The challenge stirred the imagination of artists everywhere, and paintings arrived from far and wide. Finally, the great day of revelation arrived. The judges uncovered one peaceful scene after another, while the viewers clapped and cheered.

The tensions grew. Only two pictures remain veiled.

As the judge pulled the cover from one, a hush fell over the crowd.

A mirror smoothly reflected lacey, green birches under the soft wash of the evening sky along with the grassy shore a flock of sheep grazing undisturbed. Surely this was the winner. The man with the vision uncovered the second painting himself, and the crowd gasped in surprise. Could this be peace?

A tumulus waterfall cascaded down a rocky precipice; the crowd could almost feel it's cold, penetrating spray. Stormy gray clouds threatened to explode with lightning, wind, and rain. In the mists of the thundering noises in the bitter chill, a spindly tree clung to the rocks at the edge of the falls.

One of its branches reached out in front of the torrential waters as if foolishly seeking to experience its full power.

A little bird had built a nest in the elbow of that branch. Content and undisturbed in her stormy surroundings, she rested on her eggs. With her eyes closed and her wings ready to cover her little one, she manifested peace that transcends all earthly turmoil.[1]

Peace With Self

Being at peace in the Palace takes on some interesting aspects. Peaceful living could be described by some as boring or stoic. But peaceful living has to do with contentment from within. Now peace comes from knowing that all is well, and all is being handled by the King. This does not mean we have no responsibility. We have already talked about all the kingdom inhabitants having purpose and worth, and that everyone is valued.

Peaceful palace living has to do with knowing that the King will supply all your needs according to His riches. Knowing that all your needs will be met brings great contentment. My soul also rests in the here and now and forever. Why stress? We are His people; He will take care of us. He has promised to never leave or forsake us. We should be at rest.

---

[1] Berit Kjos, A Wardrobe from the King, pp.45-46

Peace with Others

When we understand he wants everyone to live in the palace, we can see why we should not argue and fight with those, not in the palace. Why would anyone want to come into the palace if we are all fighting?

Being at peace with self and others shows a better way. Jesus said if you are hit on one cheek, turn the other cheek. When we exemplify the first key, love and joy, peace will follow. Peacefulness exemplifies Palace Life. Being at peace with others is not always easy but it is right.

Knowing Our King and Our Place in His Kingdom Brings Peace.

When you know the King personally you are at peace. Having a personal relationship talking and walking with the King day by day makes us more like Him, peaceful and at ease. Knowing we are followers, and He is the leader keeps us in the right path to follow for a peaceful life. Getting outside our proper roles and thinking we are the leaders can lead to war. War with others because we think we are more important than they are. War with self because we start thinking we know what's best for us. Even war with the King because we forget who *He* is and who we are.

We may be joint heirs to the throne, but we are not King and ruler. We must know our place, and never forget it. The only place we should ever be at war is with the enemy. This enemy is not flesh and blood but the power and principalities of the air. Satan is the Palace Dweller's enemy, and we should never listen to his lies nor ever sign a peace treaty with him. For us in the palace we must not war against ourselves, others, or the King; but with the evil one who is like a roaring lion, seeking whom he may devour.

Peacekeeper or Peacemaker

There are those who just roll with the flow agreeing with everything, thinking to be at peace. They believe we must never stand for anything. But you can never have the true peace until you know, yes know, what the palace truth is, and you stand by it. Today we have many who want to tell you what the truth is, but the word says, He, the Holy Spirit will lead you into all truth.

The peacemaker tries to appease everyone about everything. The peacekeeper tells what the king says and that each man hears as the spirit leads. Some may hear the message about tithing, giving, and offerings; some may not. It is not our job to make everyone do the King's will. It is our job to speak and take a stand for truth and let the Holy Spirit convict hearts. Recognize we are not at odds with others. They or we may be at odds with the truth.

Some may hear the message about tithing and giving offerings and think, "I need to give 10% first, then give offerings secondly as the Holy Spirit guides. Some hear the same word but come to understand that everything belongs to the King, so they give 90% and live off 10%. Some have nothing—no money, but they give time and talent, all that they have to the King. None of these are wrong, all have merit in the Kingdom.

The key is to be at peace with one's giving. If you give with the wrong attitude, you are not at peace. If you give what you have left over, you are not at peace. If you take care of yourself first, you are not at peace and then the King may just say, "If you are going to take care of yourself, you don't need me" and withdraw His hand of blessing from your life. I hope we are at peace with our giving and at peace with ourselves and others and God (The King).

Peace Comes through Strength

Peacefulness is not the same as not caring. It is knowing that the King has all the affairs of the kingdom and all its citizens in his care, therefore I can be at peace. Being strong, in your faith of the King, gives you real peace. I don't know about the future, but I know who holds the future. Now being at peace and staying at peace are two different things for be assured the enemy never wants the kingdom citizens to stay at peace. For he is a never resting enemy seeking to destroy the Palace Life. But you <u>can</u> be at peace for our King has defeated him. We very much need to let go and let God in every aspect of our lives. Not understanding why things happen we often start to think we know how things should be, but in the scheme of eternity we would have no idea if a child should live or die, if cancer should exist - or any other disease for that matter. But when we see what comes out of tragedies, we sometimes get a glimpse of the King at work. So be at peace. Don't worry; we are secure, we are safe. The King has promised it. Don't doubt the King and don't count on your power but His. *"I know the plans I have for you saith the Lord."* Jeremiah 29:11.

IT IS ALL HIS POWER, NOT OURS

When we are peace with the knowledge, it's not about what we can do. It's all about what He can do through us and with us when we are loyal Kingdom Citizens. When we focus on Him and not on ourselves, we can accomplish anything because it is the Spirit which enables us to do far more than we can ever do ourselves. The boy with the five loaves and two fish in Luke 9, did the natural. He gave all he had to the master, then our King took what was given and fed the multitude. So, we do the natural, and God does the supernatural. Knowing "He can do all things" this should give us a peace that passes all understanding. Contentment. True Peace

Commitment and courage, bring more confidence(faith) in the King and this faith brings a peace that the world cannot give, and the world cannot take away. The old song says I've got confidence in God, God is going to see me through, no matter what the case may be, I know he's going to be there for me. Palace living is peaceful living because of the king's ability, not ours.

He promises to love unconditionally.

He promises to forgive.

He promises to answer when we call.

He promises to lift us up.

He promises to strengthen us.

He promises us health.

He promises us blessings.

He promises the abundant life.

And He keeps His promises.

Praise God we can live in peace with nature itself, with other,s and with the King.

Yes! There is peace in Palace Living!

Chapter 4

> *With all lowliness and meekness, with longsuffering, forbearing one another in love.*
>
> Ephesians 4:2

KEY #4 "SUFFERING"

LONG-SUFFERING - WE CAN MAKE IT

I know there are many that think all this talk about abundant life or palace living is not realistic. They will say I have suffered, and I know others who have suffered. I don't pretend suffering doesn't exist, but we need to think, what do we learn from suffering? Do we learn how to care? Do we learn how to love those who are in need? Can we have abundant palace life in the midst of suffering? Yes! But it is not always easy! Here are some tips:

1. Don't concentrate on the problem.

2. Rely on the promises of the King never to give you more than you can handle.

3. Rely on His strength not yours.

4. Share one another's burdens.

5. Give the King glory in all things.

6. Remember (this one is hard) it's not about you.

The King allows this for our benefit to teach us or someone else to live by faith not by sight. Remember the story of Job? If you have not read it, do so. It will help you see a beautiful picture of suffering long and hard. Job's suffering has helped me and many believers for centuries. I am sure Job did not see that when he was in his deepest sorrow. This one thing for sure—we can make it with the King's help.

He Never Fails

Just because we can't see what good that suffering brings, we have the King's promise that all things work together for the good to those who love God and are the called according to His purpose. Kingdom Citizens remember that the King can't fail. He never has and never will. So, when the King closes off part of the palace, we may look at this as though He failed to take us into that new area, but in fact, it was a dangerous place to be at that time and He was protecting us. What if part of the palace wall falls? We may think failure but again we would be wrong.

Just as Nehemiah brought people together and learned to depend on God, so we too can learn and be brought closer together. Don't look at things as failures but opportunities to enhance Palace Living. I could fill an entire book of things in my life that I thought were failures but in reality, it was God taking me to new areas of Palace Living that I wasn't ready for before. He took me where I never had been before. He will do the same for you.

The King Only Allows Good For Us

Even things that taste bad can be good for us. Now even though we may think otherwise, the King does not allow things that will destroy us. (Unless the things in us are of the enemy.) That means some time we have to go through the valley so we can go up to the mountaintop. So, people we must know the King is not going to destroy His own subjects; that is a lie from the enemy. If bad things occur, hold on, the King is coming. If you get a bad report from the doctor, you will be made well either here or in the life to come but He will do what's best for you and His Kingdom.

> I lost my job—He's still King!
>
> I'm sick—He is still King!
>
> My spouse left me—He is still King!
>
> My kids don't listen—He's still King!
>
> I'm in pain—He is still King!

He will hear our cry and heal, forgive and restore us. Why? Because He can. <u>He</u> is King.

FOR IN HIM, THERE IS ALWAYS HOPE.

We may get tired or weary in well-doing but we must keep our eyes on the King. He is where our hope comes from. Our hope comes from the Lord maker of heaven and earth. He is the provider, the lifter of our head. When we put our hope in Him, we place it in the perfection of his will. When we place hope in other places, it is false hope, for no one else can do what our King can do. In Him we live in move and have our being. In him we have true hope for a brighter tomorrow, based upon His promises. One of the greatest hymns ever written says, "My hope is built on nothing less than Jesus' blood and righteousness." "On Christ the solid rock I stand all other ground is sinking sand. *All other ground is sinking sand.*"

Hope placed in man is failing.

Hope placed in possessions is failing.

Hope placed in science is failing.

Hope placed in anything other than Him is failing.

Don't ever give up hope, for in the King's name we are always hopeful.

Chapter 5

> *Who is a God like unto thee, that pardons iniquity, and passes by the transgression of the remnant of his heritage? he retains not his anger forever, because he delights in loving kindness.*
>
> Micah 7:17

KEY #5 "KINDNESS"

Whistle While you Work

In the Disney classic, Snow White and the Seven Dwarfs, the dwarfs sang and whistled the song "Whistle While You Work" creating an everlasting memory. Working with a kindness in your heart will bring Palace Living even when we are working hard. The hymn *We'll Work Till Jesus Comes*, reminds us that Palace Living still requires work.

Palace work never ends until the King says so. Keeping a kind spirit while we do his will is an absolute must so that others see what a joy palace work can be. Don't get me wrong. Work is work but when we understand the work and its importance for eternity we will work with a new joy. Every time a new person comes from the pond to the Palace, we are gaining kingdom workers to work till Jesus comes. The Word says the harvest is great, but the laborers are few.

We need to be Kingdom builders and we won't do that if the work is not done with kindness. So, let's all whistle while we work, so others will see that working for the King brings joy and kindness.

Work Together in the Kingdom

All of us need to work together. Unfortunately, too many of our churches and parachurch organizations are lone cowboys and just doing what they believe is important for their ministry growth. Jesus never started a religion or a church. He came to reestablish the kingdom. He said to pray, Thy kingdom come, Thy will be done, on earth as it is in Heaven. We must all learn to be more Kingdom minded instead of ministry minded. (or as I like to say, more kingdom building instead of castle building) Now, I know it is not always easy working across denominational lines. Sometimes some will even teach us that their interpretation is right, and everyone else's is wrong, causing them to not work outside their own denomination. This is not biblical, nor is it going to help kingdom building. It hurts palace living when we don't work for common kingdom goals. Remember we should be at peace with all in the Kingdom. Alone we can do something but together we can do much, much, more. Working together shows unity in the Kingdom or the unity of Palace Dwellers.

Right after the 9/11 attacks we came together as a nation. We still had our differences, but we came together on the belief that we were all Americans. It's not wrong to take a doctrinal stand, as matter of fact you should know what you believe and why. But if it stops you from working to bring the lost sheep into the fold or to start living this abundant life Jesus told us to live, then you are missing your purpose - to bring pleasure to the King to build up Kingdom values and principles and live by them is what Palace Living is all about. Together we should be about our Father's, the King's business; sharing His light in the darkness and helping to lead others into Palace Living. Let's work together for the glory of the King. That is what Palace Living looks like, working together with kindness.

You Reap What You Sew

Palace Planting

If you plant it, it will grow. Whatever is planted, that's what grows. You don't plant an orange tree and get a grapefruit. You will always get what you plant. If you don't plant, you won't get anything. If you plant kindness, you get kindness. If you plant evil, you will reap evil. If you plant negativity, you will get negativity. What are we planting? In the Palace the King has good soil. The King promises whatsoever we do shall prosper. If we plant in the Kingdom (let's call it Palace Planting), we will see a bountiful harvest. Not because we are great farmers but because the King promised, if we plant in good soil, we will reap Kingdom prosperity.

When Jesus taught the parable of the seed and the sewer, he showed us sometimes seed is mis-planted, therefore we get poor results. However, in Palace Planting we are guaranteed powerful, prosperous, plentiful proceeds, yes guaranteed.

So, let's start being a good Palace Dweller, planting in the kingdom where we get eternal dividends. This is our greatest opportunity to see bountiful blessings.

Chapter 6

> *How great is your goodness which you have stored up for those who fear you?*
>
> Psalm 31

KEY #6 "GOODNESS"

GOODNESS

*G*oodness and kindness go hand in hand. We must realize being good is not what gets us into the Palace, but Palace Dwellers must have goodness as a part of their character makeup.

COOPERATION IN THE KINGDOM

The human body is a great example of co-operational aspects of Kingdom advancement. In the beginning God created all things to work in perfect harmony. Animals, plants, environment, and man, working perfectly as designed, but because of man's choice we now have disharmony. When we receive Christ the Messiah and become kingdom citizens and Palace Dwellers we will begin to see more of His true harmony in our lives. God is good and what He has created is good.

The human body when operating by design will heal itself in many ways, from cuts and bruises to internal infections and even diseases. Many times, when the body is operating in harmony with proper rest, vitamins, minerals nutrition and exercise the body will repair itself. However, because the rest of the world is no longer in perfect harmony there will be times that environmental, chemical, man-made, and other outside influences that are in disharmony with one another, will cause us to be sick in body, mind or spirit. At these times we must realize this is not what God wants. He wants goodness in the Kingdom.

With Adam abundant life was lost, but in Christ abundant life, Kingdom living, can be restored. The good life is Kingdom Living. Good days—this is the day the Lord has made; I will rejoice and be glad in it. Good friends (Jesus calls us friends not servants).

Good surroundings and good living (our King blesses us out of his abundance).

Kingdom <u>health</u>

Kingdom <u>wealth</u>

Kingdom life, all of the King's <u>goodness</u> is ours as citizen as we will read in chapter 12. He is good to us, even though we don't deserve it.

GOODNESS IS POSSIBLE WITH GOOD INGREDIENTS

Good ingredients, good product. We must put good things in our spirit to expect good things out. As I said earlier, "You reap what you sow." Goodness will come out when good things are put in. The Word of God in, the Word of God out. The promises of God in, the promises of God out. We can never put evil in and expect goodness out. When we see evil coming out, we know this was not planted in the Kingdom, for in the Kingdom, everything reflects the King. Because of His goodness all things brought forth from this Kingdom will glorify him (the King), good King, good thing.

If God is good, why do bad things happen to good people? This is one of the questions people want answered. Before we look at it, we must say this. Trust God in all things. God does not answer to you. The King rules—not like a republic. What He says goes, period! Having said that we may speculate but never question the King's authority or His ability to do what is good. To question Him means we don't really trust Him, so therefore He must explain himself.

A president needs to explain because he answers to us. God (the King) does not need to explain because He does not answer to us.

Now we may speculate just to try to see good even in the bad things. But these are just that— speculations. For instance, a Christian woman is raped, and she gets pregnant; she gives the baby up for adoption. The child grows up to cure cancer. I could give many examples, but I think you get the picture.

GET THE PICTURE

All because we may not see good or understand, we must not doubt the King's Word. He is in charge—not me, not you. Trust in Him and lean not upon your own understanding. We may not understand, but we don't have to; we just need to recognize His goodness. Lord, you are good!! Yes, we have a great, good King.

Here is an example: A young boy placed in a basket and sent floating aimlessly down the Nile River was found, trained, grew up but got kicked out of the house. He killed a soldier, spent time in exile, came home and led his people out of slavery. He gave them the law of God. Out of that law all laws have their roots.

Another example: Handicapped children teach us how to love. Down syndrome children teach us how to act.

There is a story of a race for children with special needs and when one of their fellow runners fell to the ground, all the other children stopped to help, not at all concerned with winning the race. Once all was well, they linked arms and skipped across the finish line together. Praise God! What man belittles; God exalts. God, the King, takes the ordinary to do the extraordinary!

Chapter 7

> *Be strong and courageous. Do not fear or be in dread of them, for it is the Lord your God who goes with you. He will not leave you or forsake you.*
>
> Deuteronomy 31:6

KEY #7 "FAITHFULNESS"

HIS KINGDOM IS FOREVER—IT HAS NO END.

He is faithful. "Everlasting"—now that is something. In a world of throw-away-everything mentally, it is a great comfort to know He is faithful forever. His word can be counted on from generation to generation. From now throughout eternity. His love is faithful. His mercy is faithful. Morning by morning new mercies I see, all I have needed thy hand hath provided. Great is thy faithfulness, Lord unto me!

The word of God says in Deuteronomy 7:9 *"know therefore that the Lord your God is God, the faithful God who keeps covenant and steadfast love with those who love Him and keep His commandments to 1000 generations."* And in 1st Corinthians 1:9, *"God is faithful, who has called you into fellowship with His Son, Jesus Christ our Lord."*

Yes, our God is faithful, and his Kingdom has no end."

HE NEVER GIVES UP ON ME

The opposite of faithfulness is giving up. In boxing, the boxer's corner, made up of his manager and others, can throw in the towel. This is basically saying "we give up", "we quit" or "we don't have faith that victory is possible." Sometimes when that happens, the boxer is upset. He still had faith he could turn the match around and be victorious, while his corner felt otherwise.

As citizens of the Palace, we must come to realize that if our King is for us, who can be against us? Our faithfulness in Him is directly related to our acknowledgement of His faithfulness to us. He never gives up on His children. He never abandons His citizens; He never runs away from taking care of the people of the Palace.

We sometimes quit or give up on our responsibility of being a child of the King. We even shirk our duties as Palace Dwellers, but He will never give up on us. Why then, should we give up on Him? Why do *we* give up?

First, we forget that so many of God's feasts were instituted as a memorial or remembrance of something we should never forget.

Forgetting is common. In this age, many have forgotten or never known our country's history or the history of the Hebrews. Even though our salvation is not based on our knowledge of Hebrew history, or our celebrating certain feasts or Holy Days, it would do us all well, as Palace Dwellers, to know and understand what each of these feasts stood for and how Messiah was faithful to complete each one.

His faithfulness in fulfilling them is but another proof of Him being faithful in His promises to us. Never forget who our King is and who we are in Him.

The second reason we often give up is that quitting is easier than finishing. Today we are told that we deserve everything without working for it. Now, I know salvation is a gift we receive by the grace of God-through faith, not by works, lest anyone should boast. However, once we are forgiven and we are welcomed into the Palace Living through the Holy Spirit, we are now workers in the Kingdom. We should be about our Father's (The King's) business! What He gives us to do, He will enable us to finish. *He who began a good work in you, is faithful to complete it.* He will never give us more than we can handle. Even when it seems tough, don't give up. God will bring the victory because He is <u>always</u> faithful.

The third reason we quit is we get sidetracked. Getting off target can be an attack of the enemy, or because of us. Either way, we quit. We start looking around and take our eyes off the goal. We say, "I will get back to that later." Procrastination has been the enemy of many Palace Projects. What the King lays out for us to do, we need to give priority. Keeping our eyes on Him will help us to remain faithful.

The fourth reason we give up is fear.

FEAR of failure

FEAR of the enemy

FEAR of consequences

No one loves to fail, but we must remember that failure becomes success when we learn from it. If we are learning, we are growing. If we are growing, we are succeeding. If we are succeeding, we can't be failing.

Don't be afraid of success! Fear comes from the enemy. Be reminded that at the Name of Jesus, Satan MUST flee. We are "more than conquerors" for *"greater is He that is in us, than he that is in the world."* Never let fear get the best of you. Stand firm on His Word. Pray without ceasing. We are overcomers. We need to be more like Nehemiah.

Few people are familiar with the **Biblical figure Nehemiah,** and yet he was instrumental in the rebuilding and reestablishment of Jerusalem in the fifth century B.C. following the **Babylonian exile.** Although there is no consensus about the relative chronologies of the Books of Ezra and Nehemiah (the Biblical dates are unclear), Nehemiah's return to Jerusalem probably preceded Ezra's by a couple years. Both men worked together to restore the city and rededicate its people to God.

Nehemiah was a high official in the Persian court of King Artaxerxes I at the capital city of Susa, which lay 150 miles east of the Tigris River in what is now modern Iran. Nehemiah served as the king's cupbearer (Nehemiah 1:11), which evidently put him in a position to speak to the king and request favors from him. After hearing about the sad state of affairs in Judah, Nehemiah acquired the king's permission to return to Jerusalem and rebuild the city and its fortifications. He is even given letters from the king to ensure safe passage and to obtain timber from the king's forest for the gates and walls of Jerusalem.

Nehemiah returned to Jerusalem in 445 B.C. as the provincial governor of Judah/Yehud. He immediately surveyed the damage to the entire city on his well-known night journey around the walls (Nehemiah 2:12–15). He enlisted the help of the people to quickly repair the breaches in the wall. He also urged them to set up guards to defend against the constant threat of those who opposed their efforts, including the armies of **Samaria, the Ammonites** and the Ashdodites. As governor, Nehemiah says that he didn't take advantage of food and land allotments that were allowed him due to his office, because there was already such a great burden on the people of his province (Nehemiah 5:14–19)[2].

He also made the other nobles and officials forgive all outstanding debts and ordered them to return all land and money that had been taken as taxes so the people would be able to feed themselves and their families. The hurried work of repairing and rebuilding Jerusalem's walls and gates was completed in just 52 days (Nehemiah 6:15). When we remain faithful, remember His promises, when we don't quit, don't get sidetracked and when we defeat fear, (with faith) when we persevere—WE WILL OVERCOME!

This is how we remain faithful. We are overcomers because He says we are. We are overcomers because His promises are true. We are overcomers because He has overcome the world. We are overcomers because the Holy Spirit lives in us. Thank you, God, for faithfulness.

Here is a reminder from the Hymn, <u>Great is Thy Faithfulness.</u> *Great is Thy faithfulness, O God, our Father. There is no shadow of turning with thee. Thou changest not, Thy compassions they fail not. As Thou has been, Thou forever will be.*

Hallelujah!

---

[2] Willette, D. (August 21, 2021) Nehemiah-The Man Behind the Wall, Biblical Archeology Society

Chapter 8

A gentle answer turns away wrath, but a harsh word stirs up anger.

Proverbs 15:1

KEY #8 "GENTLENESS"

HE GENTLY CALLS US INTO HIS PRESENCE.

Gentleness comes from inner peace, and that inner peace comes from the spirit within. The adage "no God, no peace; know God, know peace." In other words, inner peace that brings gentleness, is a proof of the indwelling of the Spirit. His presence in us is revealed through our gentleness. Now, does that mean you will always have a gentleness about you? No. Jesus turned the tables over in the Temple throwing the money changers out of His house. Does this mean He lost it with them? No! He sat down, fashioned a whip, then told them, "You have turned my house (the house of prayer) into a den of thieves."

If we had thieves in our home, I think we would have to agree what He did was calm. He did not strike them dead! He did not beat them senseless! He simply drove them out.

There may be times when we too find ourselves in situations where we must be stern but loving and perceived as gentle. The Spirit brings this to us, we cannot do it on our own.

With all the violence that surrounds us each day, we must consistently ask the Lord to give us a gentle spirit. Palace living then becomes a life of calm gentleness.

Abundant Life is Gentle

When we are at ease with ourselves and when we are at ease with others, and when we are at ease with the King, we will be gentle. When we understand the "abundant life" we have in the Palace and we walk in that abundance, we are more at ease in life. This does not mean you will never have stress, but it does mean that the King's desire for Palace Dwellers is ease of spirit and gentleness of life.

This gentleness will be recognized by others inside and outside the Palace. They will notice that Palace Dwellers are easy going and gentle, not a stressed-out mess. The gentleness to others will be inviting. They will want to know where this gentle spirit comes from.

The Word says, "Be wise as serpents and gentle as a dove." The dove symbolizes purity. Doves were used by the poor in sacrifices at the Temple. The dove is a harmless creature, not a bird of prey. The turtle dove sings to welcome Spring. The symbolization of the dove is used to help us grasp the concept of gentleness of the Spirit.

The Holy Spirit is described as a dove. So, then Palace Dwellers (with the Spirit) are gentle as a dove. Palace Dwellers should not, I repeat should not, leave a trail of destruction in our wake, (hurt people, broken promises, division). Palace Dwellers should bring healing, restoration, and forgiveness. not pain and chaos.

Key #8 "Gentlness"

EASY TO TALK TO

Gentleness also brings an ease to communication. Not only with the King, but with other Palace Dwellers as well. It may not always make it easier to communicate with those outside the Palace as their speech and references may be different. For instance, Palace Dwellers use Biblical references, while others do not.

OUTSIDE THE PALACE	INSIDE THE PALACE
lucky	blessed
rich	prosperous
lifestyle	fulfillment
choice	freedom
relativity	right and wrong
lust, sex	love
happy	joy
gratuity	offering
government rule/anarchy	freedom in Christ
man's authority	Kingdom authority

The list could go on and on but my goal here is just to show why it is sometimes hard to talk to others about Kingdom Principles. It is with a kind gentle spirit that we can overcome our differences and shine His light. That spirit will also help us to get along with those inside and outside the Palace. Remember, the scripture tells us to be wise as serpents, but gentle as doves.

Listen More, Talk Less.

When we learn to listen, we better communicate the love of God and how wonderful life in the Palace can be. Each of us can reach different groups of people with the abundant life message. We need to be aware of the language barrier, but most of us probably already speak like we live outside the palace.

Throughout our history, we have seen that misunderstandings have consequences. Wars between nations, divorce, broken families, neighborhoods divided over politics, and racial tensions make communication even harder because of us not listening to each other.

Gentleness is necessary for us to truly care enough to really listen to people that might not agree with us on these issues. Gentleness is the most effective filter for our ears. It gives us the ability to take the most negative statements—ones that may be very offensive and possibly spoken with hatred and disgust and hear the hurt and pain of that person. when we dwell in the Palace, we speak and listen with gentleness. Gentleness is common in the Palace; therefore, good listening is the evidence of gentleness. As we listen with this gentle spirit, we can get along better with those around us.

Chapter 9

For God hath not given us the spirit of fear; but of power, and of love, and of a sound mind.

2 Timothy 1:7

KEY #9 "SELF CONTROL"

SELF-RULE

As we look at this next characteristic of Palace living, we see one that may be overlooked by some of us. However, in overlooking, we would miss one of the most important characteristics of Palace life. You see, we all must exude self-control because the King does not want to spend His time keeping the citizens in line. We must follow willingly and whole-heartedly.

Self-rule means that the ultimate responsibility for our actions is oneself. We seem to live in a world that always wants to blame others for their own bad behavior. Yes, there are enemies of the Kingdom, and enemies of the Palace life that do not want us to live the "Abundant Life." Satan is the enemy of our soul, and he tries to tell us that this life is impossible, but we know according to the Scripture that "all things are possible to those who believe."

The Palace peace is brought about by the spirit of self-control. We must live in an attitude of patience. We must let go of stress and strife which will lead us into chaos and out of control. We need to recognize that we are responsible for our own actions, and we are accountable to the King.

Life in the Palace for us is better, but sometimes makes others bitter. When we live this abundant life, as blessed and prosperous citizens of the Kingdom, others may get a little upset. This is where we need to exhibit self-control. It is hard to be blessed beyond compare and humble at the same time. If we remember that we are blessed to *be* a blessing; to be a river and not a lake; to allow blessings to flow through us—then others will perceive that our blessed life in the Palace can be theirs as well.

Self-control helps us keep our blessed life in the right perspective. The following story will illustrate this for us.

Second Kings 7 tells a fascinating story of four lepers who sat at the gate of Samaria at a time when the city was under siege. Things had gotten so bad inside the city that women were eating their own children to survive. But Elisha the prophet had predicted something that seemed utterly impossible, that the next day food would be plentiful and affordable in Samaria.

Meanwhile, the four lepers evaluated their dismal situation. If they stayed at the gate of Samaria, they would starve. If they went over to the enemy camp, they may be killed, which would be no worse than starving. But there was the outside chance that the enemy would take pity on them and give them some scraps of food.

So, they took their chances and went over to the enemy camp.

When they got there, they were shocked to find the camp deserted. The Lord had caused the enemy to hear the sound of a great army of chariots and horses so that they fled in a panic, leaving all of their supplies behind. The four beggars ate all that they could eat. They hauled away and hid several loads of silver and gold and clothes.

But then their consciences began to gnaw at them. They said, "We're not doing right. This is a day of good news, but we are keeping silent" (2 Kings 7:9). So, they went and told the starving city where they could find abundant supplies to satisfy their needs.

That story illustrates the main message of Zechariah 8, summed up by the Lord's words in verse 13:

"I will save you that you may become a blessing."

God's people are blessed to bless others. God pours out His grace on us so that we will slop it over onto others who are starving and dying without hope.[3]

We must realize we are not of greater importance to the King than anyone else who lives in or outside the Palace. Our lives, however, will operate more efficiently. Kind of like a well-oiled machine that will work better and be more efficient than one that is not well greased. This doesn't mean that Palace Dwellers will never have problems, it is just that we are able to navigate them better.

---

[3] Dunn, Jeff, "Blessed to Bless" pursuing-God.com, June 12, 2019

WHAT DOES ABUNDANT LIFE UNDER CONTROL LOOK LIKE?

Palace Dwellers tend to think right. I know, some will say, "Isn't right thinking a matter of opinion?" Not really. Right thinking is thinking that lines up with the King's decrees. That kind of right thinking is something we must work on continually.

Proverbs 23:7 *"For as he thinks in his heart, so is he. "Eat and drink!" he says to you, but his heart is not with you."*

It doesn't come naturally, but the more we are around the King, His people, His Word—the more natural it becomes for us. Thinking the right way about who He is and who we are in Him helps us to correctly evaluate the world and our place of influence in it. He is Lord, Creator and King of all, and we are His people and the crown of His creation. We have been made to be joint heirs with Jesus which makes us all part of the Royal family! That is why we can live in the Palace and not just around the Palace.

Romans 8:17, *"And if children, then heirs; heirs of God, and joint-heirs with Christ; if so be that we suffer with him, that we may be also glorified together."*

Thinking right will help us to act appropriately when life's challenges arise. Acting right is not always acknowledged by people outside the Palace as a good thing. Doing the principled thing over the popular thing is not accepted by everyone. Remember, we are not living in the Palace for our pleasure or to please others, but only to please the King. There is a song that says, "Every move I make I make in you, you make me move Jesus!" Yes, every move, every step of the journey we take direction and purpose from the Lord (King). He guides our every step. The speed we move can vary but our direction stays steady, always moving closer to Him.

The Right Story

Philippians 4:8, "*Whatsoever things are true, whatsoever things are noble whatsoever things are right, whatsoever things are pure, whatsoever things are lovely, whatsoever things are admirable* – **THINK ON THESE THINGS!**

Sometimes we let our minds go to the wrong place. Like this golf story of mine. I had just preached a sermon about positive thinking and speaking and was put to the test later that day on the course. I was golfing with my friend Vince and on the eighth hole, I hit a great shot. Using my 8 iron, I hit the ball about 134 yards. The flag was in the middle of the green, so maybe it was 140 yards. We saw the ball roll on the green but then it disappeared. We asked, "Where did it go?" We both assumed that the ball had fallen off the back of the green. I was angry. Then the Holy Spirit gently reminded me to "think right." Why do we always think the worst? So as the Spirit prompted me, I said to Vince, "No, I bet it is in the cup."

We had been golfing with a similar type of golf balls, so before we started the game, we wanted to personalize our golf balls. I put a smiley face on mine.

As we approached the green, I again said, "It's in the cup!" When I reached the flag, I looked down into the cup and saw the smiley face looking up at me. A hole in one! My very first eagle and I had a witness. It just got better from there. You see, when I walked up, I could have walked up to the hole from any direction, but I walked up at the right angle so that when looking down into the cup, my ball was facing me and smiling up at me. It could have landed face down, but it was sitting face up. A hole in one, the ball facing the right way, me walking up at the right angle.

My King was teaching me that what I thought, I already knew. Think right!!! Don't allow your mind to automatically go to the wrong placed. "I missed." "I failed." "Boo-hoo!" We do it all the time and we need to stop. The King has decreed that all things work together for good for those who love the lord and are the called according to His purpose." Get rid of the stinken' thinkin'!!! It's in the cup!

WORK RIGHT

Yes, there is lots of work in the Palace and no, it is not all preaching, teaching, or writing. Sometimes things need to be done that we don't ever like to do.

In his book *The 21 Infallible Laws of Leadership*[4], John Maxwell says we should concentrate on the things we do pretty well to raise them to an excellent level. The things at which we are poor, we should delegate. Why? Because if

---

[4] John Maxwell, The 21 Infallible Laws of Leadership

you work really hard, you may only increase your ability 2 levels. So why work to move from a 2 to a 4 in something we are not good at doing, when you could work and move from a 7 to a 9 in something you are good at. People don't look to 4's for leadership, but they do look to 9's!

This is a great lesson, however, sometimes the 9's are not available, but the 4's are willing and able. Sometimes people are inspired to work together and the 4's X 4's = 16. The Scripture puts it this way. Leviticus 26.8 - ...*and five of you shall chase an hundred, and an hundred of you shall put ten thousand to flight: and your enemies shall fall before you by the sword.* There are powerful Palace promises in numbers. It tells us that we can do some of the work alone, or we can join and accomplish much. *Work for the night cometh when we will be unable to work.*

Working right can also mean working with the right expectation. Remember, it is not up to us to fix everyone, we just need to be dedicated to the King. The Holy Spirit will bring conviction.

When we have high expectations that God will do great things, we will never be disappointed. When we have high expectations in our own ability, we are often let down and disappointed. This doesn't mean that we should not work hard but is important to work right. In Him all things are possible. Not all things are possible through us. The greatest results sometimes come from the weakest citizens who work through His authority and power.

It is His will that we work right, with integrity, wisdom, and character. We must do all our work as unto the King—only our best! Not half-hearted, lazy, weak, passionless, but our very best. I like Wesley's reply when asked the secret to his great success in drawing crowds to hear him speak. His reply was, "I set myself on fire with enthusiasm and people come from all around to watch me burn."

Working right means working with passion, energy, and perseverance. Remember, you can't work right by working wrong. In other words, citizens of the Palace must remember that if they get work done the wrong way, they bring shame to the King. Let's whistle while we work. It feels good to do a job right. We all want to hear the words, "Well done, thy good and faithful servant."

Living right is more of a state of being. It is common for Palace Dwellers to say that living right has its rewards. It is somewhat like saying when you always tell the truth, you never have to remember what you said. When people live right, they speak truth. It may not always be received well, but we understand that not everyone can handle the truth. We live right my making our yeas, yeas and our nays, nays.

Living right also means being a good neighbor. Take for instance, the story of the Good Samaritan found in Luke 10:25-37.

On one occasion an expert in the law stood up to test Jesus. "Teacher," he asked, "what must I do to inherit eternal life?"

"What is written in the Law?" he replied. "How do you read it?"

He answered, "Love the Lord your God with all your heart and with all your soul and with all your strength and with all your mind and, Love your neighbor as yourself."

Key #9 "Self Control"

"You have answered correctly," Jesus replied. "Do this and you will live."

But he wanted to justify himself, so he asked Jesus, "And who is my neighbor?"

In reply Jesus said: "A man was going down from Jerusalem to Jericho, when he was attacked by robbers. They stripped him of his clothes, beat him and went away, leaving him half dead. A priest happened to be going down the same road, and when he saw the man, he passed by on the other side. So too, a Levite, when he came to the place and saw him, passed by on the other side. But a Samaritan, as he traveled, came where the man was; and when he saw him, he took pity on him. He went to him and bandaged his wounds, pouring on oil and wine. Then he put the man on his own donkey, brought him to an inn and took care of him. The next day he took out two denarii[e] and gave them to the innkeeper. 'Look after him,' he said, 'and when I return, I will reimburse you for any extra expense you may have.'

"Which of these three do you think was a neighbor to the man who fell into the hands of robbers?"

The expert in the law replied, "The one who had mercy on him."

Jesus told him, "Go and do likewise."

Living right includes giving right and praying right. Citizens living the Palace life give with the right heart. In the book, [5]*33 Laws of Stewardship*, the author reminds us that everything belongs to God, (the King) and it is <u>all</u> His. He allows us to be stewards of what belongs to Him. Many times, we hear a word on tithing (10% given to the Lord) Many believe they have done a great deed. In truth, the King allows us to be stewards of 90%, the 10% belongs to Him. We incorrectly believe that the 10% belonged to us in the first place and we say we gave a tithe. Ten percent should be the minimum we give back.

I believe the King wants to see how we use the 90%. How we spend will paint a vivid picture of what is important to you. Luke 12:34 tells us that "for where your treasure is, there your heart will be also." Palace citizens who are wise with the 90% and don't look at the 10% as an end, but the beginning. This is not just for money. Palace citizens recognize that our time, work, and resources all belong to the King. We need to look at ourselves and ask, "How am I doing as a steward of the King's resources? Is He pleased with my care of His assets and resources?

The story of three servants can serve as an example to us. Matthew 25:14-30:

"For the kingdom of heaven is like a man traveling to a far country, who called his own servants and delivered his goods to them. And to one he gave five talents, to another two, and to another one, to each according to his own ability; and immediately he went on a journey. Then he who had received the five talents went and traded with them and made another five talents. And likewise, he who had received two gained two

---

[5] John Maxwell, 33 Laws of Stewardship

more also. But he who had received one went and dug in the ground and hid his lord's money. After a long time, the lord of those servants came and settled accounts with them.

"So, he who had received five talents came and brought five other talents, saying, 'Lord, you delivered to me five talents; look, I have gained five more talents besides them.' His lord said to him, 'Well done, good and faithful servant; you were faithful over a few things, I will make you ruler over many things. Enter into the joy of your lord.' He also who had received two talents came and said, 'Lord, you delivered to me two talents; look, I have gained two more talents besides them.' His lord said to him, 'Well done, good and faithful servant; you have been faithful over a few things, I will make you ruler over many things. Enter into the joy of your lord.'

"Then he who had received the one talent came and said, 'Lord, I knew you to be a hard man, reaping where you have not sown, and gathering where you have not scattered seed. And I was afraid and went and hid your talent in the ground. Look, there you have what is yours.'

"But his lord answered and said to him, 'You wicked and lazy servant, you knew that I reap where I have not sown and gather where I have not scattered seed. So, you ought to have deposited my money with the bankers, and at my coming I would have received back my own with interest. So, take the talent from him, and give it to him who has ten talents.

"For to everyone who has, more will be given, and he will have abundance; but from him who does not have, even what he has will be taken away. And cast the unprofitable servant into the outer darkness. There will be weeping and gnashing of teeth."

We see in this parable that the master (the King) was pleased with two servants who used what he had given them to increase what had been given to them. The one who wasted the talents was rebuked and his talent was taken from him and given to the one who best used or stewarded what he was in charge of. This teaches us that the King wants us to utilize the blessing and gifts – not save them for ourselves. When God blesses you financially, don't raise your standard of living, raise your <u>standard of giving</u>!

PRAY RIGHT

Mark 9:29 teaches us to cast out demons – in Jesus' name.

John 14:13 talks about God meeting our need so the King is glorified.

Matthew 6:16-18 tells us what we should do when we fast.

I've heard it said that prayer is preparation, not appropriation. In other words, prayer is to prepare us for Palace living, not for appropriating things from the King.

Praying right means praying the King's decrees. The example prayer is found in Matthew 6:9-13:

This, then, is how you should pray:

Our Father in heaven, hallowed be your name,

your kingdom come, your will be done, on earth as it is in heaven.

Give us today our daily bread. And forgive us our debts,

as we also have forgiven our debtors.

And lead us not into temptation but deliver us from the evil one.

This example prayer tells us to recognize His authority and will above our own. To bless us each day by meeting our needs, to forgive us as we forgive others; to deliver us from the evil one.

Richard Wagner encourages people to use the following acronym when praying.

A = Adoration—give God all the Glory, Honor and Praise.

C= Confession—confess that we all sin and have weaknesses.

T= Thanksgiving—speak what you are thankful for—thanksgiving produces thanks-living!

S= Supplication—mention our needs, our concerns for others.

How to Pray Right

- We should pray for one another.

- We should pray fervently (James 5:16- ...*the effectual fervent prayer of a righteous man availeth much*).

- We should pray often (I Thessalonians 5:17...*Pray without ceasing. In everything give thanks: for this is the will of God in Christ Jesus concerning you.*)

- We should pray to keep a close relationship with the King.

If we pray as an act of communication, not only do we speak to the King, but we must also listen. Psalm 46:10...*be still and know that I am God.*

God commands us to pray right. James 4:3...*When you ask, you do not receive, because you ask with wrong motives, that you may spend what you get on your pleasures.*

- We should pray in the Spirit.

    I know this may sound mystical, but it is really simple. We know His spirit is in us. Yes, we know! when we moved into the Palace, we do so at the Father's drawing. John 6:44...*No one can come to me unless the Father who sent me draws them, and I will raise them up at the last day.*

    We can't be called by the Father to receive His Son and not have the Spirit. We can, however, be in the Palace and have the spirit but not be filled with the Holy Spirit. I know a lot of this has to do with differing terminologies, but it doesn't have to be mystical. When we pray, our spirit bears witness with the Holy Spirit. It is a spiritual connection. Not to dumb it down or oversimplify, but its like when a child is away from their mom, they can still feel her watching over them, knowing how she feels about whatever is going on, good or bad! So, pray in the Spirit.

Right praying will sometimes include fasting. Fasting and prayer go hand in hand. Fasting isn't done to show everyone how serious you are about praying; it is to show God you are serious about Him.

Leonard Ravenhill said that you can measure a church's popularity by its attendance on Sunday morning. The pastor's popularity can be measured by the attendance on Sunday night, and God's popularity is measured by attendance at Wednesday Prayer meeting! Wow, how times have changed—or have they? Most churches today only hold Sunday morning services. If they do have a Wednesday night service, they don't spend much time talking about prayer, let alone taking time to pray. Now, I am not judging, just pointing out this truth. When you move into Palace living, prayer is no longer a chore. It becomes part of everyday, all the time, everywhere, about everything. Its communication with the King all the time.

Now fasting, according to the King's decree, should not be talked or boasted about. As a matter of fact, no one should even know you are doing it. Matthew 6:16-18...*When you fast, do not look somber as the hypocrites do, for they disfigure their faces to show others they are fasting. Truly I tell you, they have received their reward in full.17But when you fast, put oil on your head and wash your face,18so that it will not be obvious to others that you are fasting, but only to your Father, who is unseen; and your Father, who sees what is done in secret, will reward you.*

Come boldly in Jesus' name and anything you ask will be given. What should we ask? Things that the King has already said. It is not His will for any to perish but come to repentance. 2 Peter 3:9...*The Lord is not slow in keeping his promise, as some understand slowness. Instead, he is patient with you, not wanting anyone to perish, but everyone to come to repentance.*

So, pray for people to get saved!

- Pray His promises

    There are literally thousands of promises. Here are just a few:

    Psalm 50:15...*and call on me in the day of trouble; I will deliver you, and you will honor me*

    Isaiah 58:6...*is not this the kind of fasting I have chosen:*

    to loose the chains of injustice and untie the cords of the yoke,

    to set the oppressed free and break every yoke?

    John 8:36...*So if the Son sets you free, you will be free indeed.*

    Ezekiel 36:26-27...*I will give you a new heart and put a new spirit in you; I will remove from you your heart of stone and give you a heart of flesh.*

    Romans 8:1-2...*Therefore, there is now no condemnation for those who are in Christ Jesus, because through*

> *Christ Jesus the law of the Spirit who gives life has set you free from the law of sin and death.*

Palace Dwellers do not live in condemnation but freedom!

He promises us that we are new creatures (2 Corinthians 5:17).

He promises we shall not fulfill the lust of the flesh (Galatians 5:16).

He promises us shelter from the enemy (Psalm 61:3).

He promises us that at His name, Satan must flee (James 4:7).

My fellow Palace Dwellers, are you now seeing that we can pray all these promises? He WILL answer because He has already said it is His will! So, when we pray <u>His Word</u>, <u>His Promises</u>, <u>His Will</u>, we are granted <u>His answer</u>. Think right and pray right. Don't ask amiss. Don't ask your will but His will be done, and it will come to pass! Decree the King's promises.

Chapter 10

> God is faithful; He will not let you be tempted beyond what you can bear.
>
> I Corinthian 10:13

KEY #10 "PROTECTION"

ABUNDANT LIFE COMES WITH PROTECTION.

As Palace Dwellers, we live this abundant life under the protection of the King. Protection is provided to us, for us, and with us. This protection by the King is not by our might or power, but by His spirit says the Lord. (Zechariah 4:6)

Our protection does not depend on our abilities or strengths, but the King's spirit which is given to all Palace Dwellers. We are protected 24/7—not just in times of war, but in times of peace as well. The enemy wants to attack us, and he will. But we are under the King's protection and need not fear. When the enemy comes in like a flood, we must remember the God of Noah. When the enemy takes shots with darts of accusation, we must remember that He is our Shield. (Psalm 28:7) He is our fortress, strong tower, our deliverer. (Psalm 144:2) Yes! He is our shelter, our refuge. He is our protector – in whom then shall we fear?

SAFE AM I—OR AM I SAFE?

Some may ask, "If we are in the Palace and safe, why then are there so many things coming against us?" The answer has a lot to do with your thinking and understanding. Some will say, "I don't feel safe or protected!!" But that doesn't change the promise that you *are safe*. Safe and protected! So how can we feel safe and protected? Again, know the truth and the truth will set you free. We must be in His Word to keep our minds set on Him. The King says I am safe, so I am safe. When I doubt my safety or protection, I am doubting the King and His promise. Now we all go through times of doubt but Romans 12:2 tells us, *"and be ye not conformed to this world*; (Am I safe?) *but be ye transformed by the renewing of your mind.* (Safe am I!) Also, John 4:4 tells us, *"Ye are of God, little children, and have overcome them; because greater is He that is in you, than he that is in the world."*

You are the King's citizens (Palace Dwellers), and you have and will overcome the attack because greater is our King than their king. We <u>can</u> know we are safe, and we can live a protected life.

ANGELS AND FELLOW SOLDIERS

Another promise of safety is that Angels have been given specific charge over us. *"He will order His angels to protect and guard us* (Luke 4:10).

Key #10 "Protection"

One of the more popular King's decrees come to us in Psalm 91:11-12. *"For He will command His angels concerning you, to guard you in all your ways. On their hands they will bear you up, lest you strike your foot against a stone."*

Sometimes, the angel is the Lord Himself. Exodus 23:20 says, *"See, I am sending an angel ahead of you to guard you along the way and bring you to the place I have prepared."*

The angels also minister to us by revealing knowledge to us. Now where does the King say that each of us has a specific guardian angel just for us, but we know that they are watching out for us, and they are all around. Here is a good reason to always show kindness to strangers: Hebrews 13:12 *"Do not forget to show hospitality to strangers, for by so doing some people have shown hospitality to angels without knowing it."*

Who then are the angels? The word angel means messenger. So, you may ask are they just here to spread the King's Word and will throughout the world?

Angels have been around before man. Satan was present as a fallen angel in the Garden. Since Satan was an angel, we can make the statement with certainty that angels have the ability to come and go from Heaven to earth. Isn't it funny that some of us feel safe because angels are looking out for us, rather than feeling safety in the King's promises? Entire books could be written on angels and their purpose in the world, but I just wanted to remind you that angels are just another way the King protects His Palace Dwellers.

SOLDIERS

2 Timothy 2:4 *No one serving as a soldier gets entangled in civilian affairs, but rather tries to please his commanding officer.*

Therefore put on the full armor of God, so that when the day of evil comes, you may be able to stand your ground, and after you have done everything, to stand (Ephesians 6:13).

There are many places in the Scriptures where we read that we are soldiers fighting in battle. But I want to make this point very clear. THE BATTLE HAS ALREADY BEEN WON! We are to occupy until the King returns.

"Have I not commanded you? Be strong and courageous. Do not be afraid; do not be discouraged, for the Lord your God will be with you wherever you go" (Joshua 1:9).

So yes, we must fight against powers and principalities and wickedness in high places— with a goal to maintain and stand.

As soldiers we also look out for one another. We must have each other's backs. Palace Dwellers should help, lift and speak life into others. So often, we attack each other instead of the enemy. Soldiers must keep vigilant—yes open and alert. Do not allow the lies of the enemy to turn you against one another. Palace Dwellers are not jealous but should be genuinely joyful for each other's successes. We should run, not walk to the defense of our fellow citizens. As good soldiers, we must not only help others, but we must also help ourselves by putting on the whole armor of God.

A soldier's armor is probably one of the most important aspects of Palace Living. Many would question why Palace

Dwellers would need to wear armor inside the Palace walls. It is simple; it is for us to feel more secure and to be ready for any attack on us or the Palace. I Peter 3:15 says, *"...But in your hearts revere Christ as Lord. Always be prepared to give an answer to everyone who asks you to give the reason for the hope that you have. But do this with gentleness and respect...*

All our Palace armor is defensive except for the Sword of the Spirit. The Sword is an offensive weapon. Soldiers can learn to use defensive weapons offensively. Let's take a look at some scripture to support this thinking.

Ephesians 6:10-18

10Finally, be strong in the Lord and in his mighty power. 11Put on the full armor of God, so that you can take your stand against the devil's schemes. 12For our struggle is not against flesh and blood, but against the rulers, against the authorities, against the powers of this dark world and against the spiritual forces of evil in the heavenly realms. 13Therefore put on the full armor of God, so that when the day of evil comes, you may be able to stand your ground, and after you have done everything, to stand. 14Stand firm then, with the belt of truth buckled around your waist, with the breastplate of righteousness in place, 15and with your feet fitted with the readiness that comes from the gospel of peace. 16In addition to all this, take up the shield of faith, with which you can extinguish all the flaming arrows of the evil one. 17Take the helmet of salvation and the sword of the Spirit, which is the word of God.

18*And pray in the Spirit on all occasions with all kinds of prayers and requests. With this in mind, be alert and always keep on praying for all the Lord's people.*

Each piece of the armor has great significance and many books have been written on the armor of God. Some of the best in my opinion are by Perry Stone who wrote <u>Putting on Your God Gear</u> and <u>The Armor of God Personal Study</u>. So, I will not try to rewrite what I feel is a great book on the armor, but I will remind you to PUT IT ON!!

WALLS

When I think about walls, my mind goes to the story of Jericho. This wall was substantial. It was built with three tiers, or layers. First, there was an earthen rampart or embankment that inclined up to the second tier—a retaining wall that was 12-15 feet high. On top of this stone wall was another wall made of mud and bricks which stood 20-26 feet high. The wall was 6 feet thick. From the bottom looking up it would seem like 10 stories high. But we know that there is no wall too high or too big that our King can't overcome. He has put walls in place to protect us, but He will knock down walls that separate us from Him.

One of those walls that separate us and keeps the citizens of the palace divided, is the denominational wall. I don't want you to think I am saying that denominationalism is terrible, but the only group inside the palace should be "Kingdom" citizens. Separate groups or clubs can cause us to be used against one another. Its like a football team. One group is the offense, the other, the defense. If someone convinces one group that they don't need the other, you cannot win. The Word says, "…a house divided against itself cannot stand (succeed, win, have victory)" Mark 3:25. So, if the offense scores every time, but the defense does not stop the opposing team from scoring, the best you could hope for is to make the last score before time runs out.

Walls that divide us inside the Palace are of a great concern. You've heard the phrase, "United we stand, divided we fall." We can see this in our country. At the time of this writing, we are more divided as a country than anytime since the Civil War. We have been deceived by the enemy that only "our group" is right. Whether it be men/women, children/older folks, conservatives/liberals, physically fit/unfit, tall/short, rich/poor…this list could go on forever. Most of these differences are personal preferences and not convictions. Not Palace principles. Let me explain.

Inside the Palace, we should be united on Palace Principles.

1. The King's laws are eternal.
2. They are not amendable (never change).
3. They are for everyone.
4. They are understood to be righteous.
5. Breaking them has consequences.
6. They are necessary and beneficial.

The Ten commandments were given to us by God and even though we live under grace, it does not mean that Palace life would not reflect these laws.

In the Palace there is no murder (the taking of a life).

There is no other King (His law is supreme).

Mothers and Fathers are to be honored by their children.

There is no thievery. No taking another's possessions or wanting what is not yours.

There is a day of rest (to worship).

There is no lying.

Jesus said it even more plainly in Luke 10:27. *"Love the Lord thy God with all your heart, and with all your soul and with all your strength and with all your mind; and love your neighbor as yourself."*

In Palace living we should have a love of the King. We should worship Him alone. We should not kill (no abortion or spilling of innocent blood). We should Honor our Father and Mother. We should create 6 days (work) and rest on the 7th day. We should be people of our word. Let your yeas be yeas and your nays be nays. We should not take or covet what is not ours, but instead covet those gifts of the King earnestly desiring what He has given to us.

We must remember the walls of the Palace are not there to keep us inside, but to separate us from the world that does not believe in the King's law or recognize His authority. We cannot expect those on the outside of the wall to agree on these things, but we should be able to agree on the inside. When the enemy deceives us and causes us to build walls on the inside, that divides us and makes us weaker and more susceptible to attacks. So instead of us showing those on the outside this great Palace life that we are inviting them to move into, we are convinced to build walls inside the Palace or move out of the Palace all together.

The walls of the Palace were never built to deter those willing to accept the King's decrees to come in and partake of the palace life. Nor were they built to lock us (citizens) in—hidden away from the outside world, but to declare His Kingship, Palace principles and promises of the Palace life.

Walls set boundaries and borders. They are not good or bad, they can be either. They are bad when we make them to have things our own way. Once we live in the Palace, our eyes are open to these differences. We can have the King's definition of love, joy, peace, goodness, kindness and faithfulness, or we can have the world's counterfeits of these, but we cannot live in the Palace and live by counterfeit decrees. God, (the King) says love God (the King) with all your heart and love your neighbor as yourself. The world says to love yourself—that it's all about you—(I want, I need, I am).

The King says He provides more than enough. Our King gives those in the Palace life—more than enough. Abundant life! Our blessings are not intended to be kept and hidden away, but we are blessed so that we can be a blessing to others. Therefore, we have all this, not because we deserve it, but because He declares it. We serve the King of Kings. What an honor! John Milton in Paradise Lost says, "It is better to rule in Hell than to serve in Heaven." How sad for those that live by these words. They are false. It is far better to be safe and secure with the King of Kings, with Palace life protections, love, joy, peace, goodness, kindness, and faithfulness than to rule in a place of death, pain, suffering and agony.

So, lets tear down the walls that divide us as Kingdom citizens. The walls of race, doctrine, distrust, culture, tradition, legalism, selfishness, and elitism. Let's live within the walls of unity, love, joy, peace, goodness, kindness and faithfulness.

Guidance

We are protected not only by angels, fellow soldiers, walls, and armor, but also by *divine guidance*.

FIRST—Guidance is delivered to us in many ways. The first and most important is the Word of the King (The Holy Bible). The King's love letter is Him speaking directly to us. We must first acknowledge that His Word is divine (Holy). We must recognize it is infallible in its original language, understanding that sometimes going through the translation process some things might be different. However, it has been studied exhaustively and no real change in meaning has occurred. His Word is the same yesterday, today, and forever. Matthew 24:35 says, *"Heaven and earth will pass away, but my words will never pass away."* It is eternal. It is all His Word, not in part, but the whole. In the words of my friend Dr. Fred Bertolet—we should believe in the whole Bible, not a Bible full of holes.

SECONDLY—Guidance is delivered to us through the correct interpretation of the Holy Word of the King. this can only happen through the precious Holy Spirit. While we can read the King's decrees and teachings, we cannot understand without the guidance of the Holy Spirit. The Holy Spirit not only guides us in the Word, but in "all" things. This guidance is crucial to our Palace living. Hearing the voice of the King through the Holy Spirit, and understanding what it means, is essential to our joyful life in the Palace.

Through the guidance of the Holy Spirit, we are led into <u>all</u> truth; we begin to grasp the wonderful promises of the King. We will look at this in the next chapter.

Guidance helps us in decision making. Whether the decision is big or small, the Holy Spirit works to guide us into all truth.

The Holy Spirit can and does guide us – whether it be a word from a nationally recognized speaker or a word from a little child. The King can use either, if we listen to that still, small voice.

THIRDLY—We are guided through Godly influence. That is why it is very, very, very, very, very, important who we allow to speak into our lives. Lucifer told Eve, "God has said…" then proceeded to twist what God had said. This type of lie continues today. Be careful of all who say, "God told me." If God truly did tell them, then it will be confirmed in Scripture. If what they say is not confirmed in God's Word, then by what authority are they declaring?

God will never go against what He has already declared. Satan said to Eve, "Surely, you will not die." But God said, "If you touch or eat of the tree in the middle of the Garden, you will die." God means what He says. Satan spins what God says by adding that Eve could be like God and know all good and evil. A partial truth is still a lie. When they followed the serpents lie, their eyes were opened and yes, they became mortal and would now experience death.

Beware if someone's teachings do not line up with God's Word, not matter how close it is, no matter how much of it is true, it is a lie! When others come to you to speak things into your life and some of those things line up with the Word of God, but some things do not – you must not be guided by them. *Thy Word have I hid in my heart, that I might not sin against thee.* Proverbs 119:11

Dreams and Visions

Much has been written on dreams and visions. I will do my best to summarize what I have learned over the years. To continue with what has already been written, DO NOT follow dreams or visions that do not line up with God's Word.

Even though we can look at Joseph's life and can see how his dreams were fulfilled, at the time he was sharing the dream with his brothers, he wasn't able to see the full picture. But by sharing his dream, he enabled generations to see how God brought His dream to fruition. Some dreams, as in the story of Joseph, happen regardless of what we do. Others spur us into action. The Tower of Babel was a vision of men trying to reach God. They might have done better had they reached toward Him with their hearts of praise and worship.

When we try to make a dream come true, we take the Glory, but also the responsibility. It is not wrong to step out by faith, but make sure you are stepping with the King and not on the King's glory. The dream that He has given to you, He will bring to pass. The dream you work to bring to pass, will always be yours to maintain. The dream He brings to pass will bless you and your descendants.

So, how are we guided by dreams? Dreams can reveal things to us through abstract ways. We must pray and seek God trough the Holy Spirit to reveal to us what is being taught. I will confess that sometimes it is God trying to get us to listen and sometimes, it's the late-night pizza. Again, always ask, "Does this line up with the Word of God. Does this bring me closer to the King?" Joseph's dream took many years to come to fruition, so don't think that if you have a dream on Monday, it will come to fruition on Tuesday.

A vision can be broad or narrow. No matter how broad or narrow, write your vision down. If God leads you to it, He will see you through it!

There is a vision which transforms. God doesn't just reform us, He transforms us into new creatures in Christ when we are saved. We move from the pond to the Palace. We begin to learn how different life is in the Palace versus the pond. We, in the pond, had dreams of a new lily pad, better bugs to eat, and more water sports to enjoy.

Once inside the Palace, our dreams and visions are about His Kingdom and His will. It is about teaching others about Palace dwelling and Kingdom life. As we fulfill His purpose, we will be blessed along the way.

The vision which transforms—transforms us from self to selfless. The vision which transforms changes our stinkin'thinkin' to the mind and heart of Christ. It is in Him that we live and move and have our being.

Our direction is guided by the visions and dreams that God

places in us. He fulfills them through His Spirit, so let go and let God! Stop trying to make it happen and let God happen in us.

Oh, that we may learn the One who gives direction and guidance just needs us to be obedient to Him. Moses was obedient and asked God. God brought the plagues, and the vision became reality. If they would have obeyed the vision sooner, things may have turned out differently.

CHAPTER 11

> *But thanks be to God, who giveth us the victory through our Lord, Jesus Christ.*
>
> I Corinthians 15:57

KEY #11 "VICTORY"

One of the great things about Palace Living is being victorious. We often say, "Let's get the victory!" Well, that is part of the problem; we don't need to get it; it (the victory) is already ours. We need to live in it and not try to get it. When we try to get it, we are saying we don't have it. All the battles have already been won. We just need to occupy the land. Knowing who we are (representatives of the King, joint heirs with Jesus) makes us princes and princesses of the throne of God. This is not meant to give us a big head, but it does put a crown on our head.

When we know who we are in Christ, we have authority when we speak because of who He is. Now this does not mean the enemy will never attack but fighting while in a secure position makes us victorious.

The world's court votes to allow abortion, or as some call it, "a woman's right to choose." The killing of innocent babies may seem to be a lost battle to Palace Dwellers. My friends hear this loud and clear. No matter what happens, whether it be the legalization of marijuana, legalizing same sex marriage, or the selling of aborted baby parts – God is still on the throne. We are still victorious because the world never gave us the victory, God did, therefore the world cannot take it away. Not by the court, not by governments, not by man's laws.

Three Hebrew boys Hananiah, Mishael, and Azariah or Shadrach, Meshach, and Abednego (Chaldean names) looked like they had lost the victory. After refusing to bow to the earthly king, they were sentenced to the fire. Did they lose the victory? They did not! Even if they had died in the fire, they never would have lost the victory. Whether they lived or died, they had the victory because faith is the victory that overcomes the world – and they had faith. When He delivered them (without even the smell of smoke on their clothing), God showed the earthly king a glimpse into the Palace of the King of Kings. And a glimpse was all he needed.

In Daniel chapter 6, Darius, King of Babylon was given a glimpse of His power when our King delivered Daniel from the lion's mouth. He gave the Israelites a glimpse of His glory and victory over the Philistines when he let little David kill Goliath the Giant with only a sling and stone. Because of their faith, they did not fight the battles – God did. They stood by faith and relished in the victory. We too can stand in the occupied territory of victory. It is ours says the Lord of hosts. The King has decreed it. It is so. So stand strong!

STAND STRONG

As we have seen thus far, this Palace life is wonderful. It is full of joy, love and peace. It is truly a blessed life.

We have also seen that the enemy is still roaming to and fro like a lion seeking to deceive, destroy and devour. He wants to take territory that does not belong to him.

We realize that we have the victory, however, we must occupy and fight when needed to keep the Palace secure. So even now the enemy is at the gate. Most Palace Dwellers may not even be aware of the enemy. They go about daily life and then when the attack comes, they are not ready. Their armor is not on. Soldiers at the wall may be ready, but not every attack will come from the outside. Some attacks may come from the inside. This is when we must stand. We must not just stand but stand strong. All (not just some) must stand together and that is what makes us undefeatable.

In Israel, everyone, at age 18, must serve in the Israel Defense Force (I.D.F.). All citizens are trained soldiers. Even when they finish their years of active duty, they remain ready to serve, keeping their weapon in good shape and are prepared if called upon to serve.

Standing strong means being steadfast and unmovable. Your feet must be firmly planted like tree roots; your legs set to give you maximum balance. When I was in the high school choir, we were taught to always keep our knees slightly bent while standing. We were warned that if we locked our knees, we could pass out. Sometimes, we stand so straight and rigid that we are more susceptible to attack. Standing strongly together makes us a force to be reckoned with.

Many Palace Dwellers have forgotten that we are still defending the King and His Kingdom every day, everywhere, all the time—inside the walls and outside the walls. We don't have to go out looking to attack, but we must always be ready to defend. What does this look like? Well, you may be the only person at your job who lives in the Palace. Those outside the Palace may even be angry with you because of your relations to the King. The Word tells us to rejoice when we are hated for His sake.

Standing could mean to speak positive about the King when everyone around you is speaking negatively. Standing could mean when others are asking us to act against the King's decrees, but we stand firm on the Palace principles.

You see, most of the time, the people who say they don't like us are not mad at us. They are mad at our King.

Standing give us insight on how we occupy. We don't gather our troops to attack, but to stand. There is a fine line between defense and offence. If someone attacks us as we stand firm in the King's decree—they might just run into our shield and knock themselves out! They may say we attacked them, but we simply stood firm. They generated the force of the blow!

As we stand firm, we do have one offensive weapon—the sword. The Word of God is our offence to fight off any attackers. We MUST know how to use it correctly. Jesus is our example. When he was tempted by Satan, Jesus used the Word of God to fight off the attack. He didn't go looking for the enemy but was ready when the enemy attacked. Prayer and fasting are the way we prepare so that when the time comes, we can stand and stand strong. Fasting should be done privately – do not boast. The Word says to wash your face so only you and God know. This means we are to prepare to stand from the inside out. We could say it this way:

>Put in your heart the armor of God.

>Put in your heart the truth of salvation.

>Put in your heart His righteousness.

>Put in your heart faith.

>Put in your heart the Gospel of peace.

Do this, so you can share the Word and stand strong.

CHAPTER 12

> The Lord reigns, let the earth be glad, let the distant shores rejoice.
>
> Psalm 97:1

KEY #12 "OUR GOD REIGNS"

Yes, we are victorious. We are strong. Now we need to take this and use it to build His Kingdom. The Palace is big enough for all who desire to come in. We need to share the good news that our God (the King) reigns. We need to share with every other kingdom that our God reigns. We need to share with all nations and with all people – our God reigns. <u>All</u> Kingdoms need to come under His influence.

HE REIGNS IN THE KINGDOM OF HEALTH

We live in a society that is very "pharmaceutical." In reality, there are many people inside and outside the Palace that use drugs. Now, I know this is one of those statements that people look at and roll their eyes. You think I'm going to tell you that all medications are evil. They are not, but it was never supposed to be this way. Our King created mankind perfect. No medications needed! But with Adam and Eve's fall from grace, our bodies have become more and more corrupt. They are no longer perfect. They still work, but just not as good. Our health is now in decline. Generation to generation our health continues to decline.

The good news is that with a good diet, exercise, and stress management, we can get a lot from our bodies. They repair themselves in miraculous ways. But, we will never be perfect again as they were in the Garden.

Some Palace Dwellers my struggle as to why there are sick among us and ask, "How does being sick or diseased bring glory to God?"

> 1. It allows us to be healed – the leper, the blindman, the deaf all brought honor to God (John 9:3).

1. It reminds us that our bodies are not as they once were – *perfect* (I Corinthians 15:22).
2. It reminds us of our weaknesses and our need for a Savior (2 Corinthians 12:9).

Here are some examples:

God allows some to be born with what the world calls brain damage. Some can't read or write or tie their shoes. They can't function alone and are unable to perform the most common tasks. However, they can hear a difficult piano concerto and immediately reproduce what they hear on the piano, never having played before. Others may have lost an arm or leg through disease or accident, and despite their loss, they go on to do great things. These examples show us how we are not using our bodies or our minds to their fullest potential.

Not all sickness is caused by the fall or sinful living, but some most certainly are. Someone who drinks excessive alcohol and develops liver disease has to recognize they are partly to blame for their condition. Some who develop lung cancer can't say they are under satanic attack if they have smoked for many years. There will always be illnesses, accidents and even deaths that we don't understand. It is not for us to know every way the King is working to bring about His plan. It is not for us to figure out but to trust in the King.

It is God's desire that we live in the Palace with great health. Kingdom health is ours. We can do the natural (diet, exercise, prescribed meds) but God (the King) is still the giver of health with the supernatural ability to heal. It is never wrong to ask the physician for help, just never forget the healing always comes through the Great Physician.

The Kingdom of Wealth

Over the years, prosperity preaching and teaching has confused many, helped some, and hurt some. I will attempt to put things in perspective from the Palace life perspective.

In the Palace, wealth is common. Kingdom living is a commonwealth society. Kingdom wealth principles work for Palace Dwellers and in most cases, non-palace dwellers as well.

Why would you listen to me? What credentials make you an authority? Well, I am over 60 years old and have lived many days. I hold three Ph.D. degrees. I've been financially responsible in both my personal and ministry life. But the real reason you should follow these principles is because they work and come directly from God. Everything belongs to God; we are only the managers of God's belongings. Hebrews 2:10-18

In this Kingdom of wealth, we understand that everything (all) belongs to Him (the King). He allows us to manage or do what we desire with 90%.

Where your treasure is, there your heart will be also (Matthew 6:21). If your heart is with the King, your treasure will be also. So lay up treasures in heaven, not on earth. Always plant seeds in Godly endeavors. If you do, it will be returned to you pressed down, shaken, and running over (Luke 6:38).

Remember that we are not like lakes that are designed to store water (blessings) rather we are reservoirs where water (blessings) come in and freely flow out. When the King gives us a full measure of blessings and we keep it, we have no room to receive any more blessings. The more we give out the more room we have for blessings. We must make sure our giving is not just happenstance but given for the purpose God has laid on our hearts—a gift from the heart is more valuable than the size of the gift.

Kingdom wealth comes about by the King's will, not the citizens work. Therefore, we must always remember our source will never run out. Keep your eyes on the King. This is where your help comes from!

We must also learn to be satisfied with what the King blesses us with. Do you remember the story of the Israelites in the wilderness? They were guided by a cloud by day and a pillar of fire by night. They had manna given to them every morning, but they wanted meat. We can identify with the

Israelites because too often we are not satisfied with what God has provided. We must learn to trust He knows best. We must think of finances as a way to do what's needed in His Kingdom, not just so we can have more "stuff."

So, lets recap:

>Remember, everything belongs to God. (Hebrews 2:10-18)
>
>We are only managers of what is His. (Chronicles 29:9-17)
>
>Freely receive, freely give. (Matthew 10:8)
>
>Plant good seed in good soil. (Matthew 6:21, Mark 4:8)
>
>Be a reservoir, not a lake. (Zechariah 8:1-23)
>
>You are blessed to be a blessing. (Genesis 12:1-3)
>
>The size of the heart, not the size of the gift is what matters. (Widow's mite offering- Mark 12:33-34)
>
>Don't lay up treasures on earth but in Heaven. (Luke 12:16)
>
>Be satisfied with what God provides. (Exodus 16)

Kingdom of Knowledge

It is very important for a Palace Dweller to have the mind of Christ. Now I don't pretend to say that every thought I have, or will have, will be the same as the King's. That's why the Word has said we should keep our hearts and minds in Christ Jesus. We must constantly look at our motives, actions, and thoughts and keep them on the King and His decrees. To do that we must "know" the truth.

What is Truth?

In today's world, we are told that truth is relative. We are told that "your" truth may not be "my" truth. Proof of that is a YouTube video where a white male, about 5'11" and 145 pounds in his mid-20's interviewed college students at the University of Washington. The students were asked, "If I told you I was really a 6'5" Chinese woman, or a 7-year-old child, would that be the truth?" "Yes," they said, it was. They were unwilling to speak truth because they have been taught to be politically correct. We, as Palace Dwellers, have an obligation to speak the truth (God's Word) into every aspect of our lives.

Many people have been deceived by the enemy that the King's laws and decrees no longer apply or are outdated. In reality, His decrees are eternal! They are the truth yesterday, today, and forever.

> *He is the *only* true King – eternal.
>
> *He created all there is, therefore, anything created in the future by us is still made from elements He created.
>
> *He created us male and female (for His glory).
>
> *He tells us to be fruitful and multiply.

*He provided a way for us to come and live in the Palace. Pond living (even with Jesus) is still not like Palace living with the Holy Spirit. We must be born again and filled with power after the Holy Ghost comes upon us.

*He provides us with gifts to enable us to be victorious. To understand the will of the King and to be effective.

*He gives us wisdom to know how to use all of this knowledge; for truly knowledge without wisdom is like a chainsaw without gas.

Knowing the truth as to why Jesus came to the earth is very important. Jesus came to bear witness or to testify to the truth. (John 18:7

Jesus came as the Lamb of God whose blood would bring salvation and take away the sins of the world. I love how this was explained at a conference I attended with the late Dr. Myles Munroe. He said that we should think of the earth as a colony of Heaven. Adam and Eve were to colonize (populate) this new place. However, through their disobedience they sinned because they listened to the lie of an unemployed cherub (Satan). But that is not the end of the story.

The King sent His son to correct and fulfill the requirements for redemption that were foretold. Jesus did just that. You see, Jesus came into Jerusalem riding on a colt on the tenth day of Nissan (we call it Palm Sunday). This is the exact day that the Passover lamb would have been taken into the Hebrew home. Everyone would spend time with the lamb.

The lamb would have been loved by the children. Then, the papa of the house would inspect the lamb and decree that it was worthy to be sacrificed.

This role was fulfilled unknowingly by Pontious Pilate when he said, "I find no fault in Him." Jesus was then crucified. Nails pierced His hands and feet. A spear poked into his side, but just like the Passover lamb, His bones were not broken. His blood flowed with water and mingled down, just as water would have been poured over the lamb to wash the blood into the catch basin. Jesus' body gave forth blood and water— the life cleansing blood.

Oh, the blood of Jesus, it will never lose its power! It flowed bringing our salvation— hallelujah.

It seems that even in the story of the passion of the Christ, His death and resurrection, the truth that He is Messiah is being twisted, forgotten, and rewritten to fit into new narratives— removing that He was the Passover Lamb for all mankind, removing that He was perfect—without spot or blemish, removing that He died at the hour that the lamb would have been sacrificed, removing His blood and teaching only that He was our great example, removing His resurrection, ascension, and return.

The truth would and is in some cases being replaced by fables for itchy ears. Re-written history like no virgin birth, no perfect life, that he was married, that His death was faked, His body stolen, His resurrection was just His spirit are being shared and believed. All these are to undermine the truth. If He was not perfect, He could not be the Passover Lamb of God. Jesus fulfilled 100's of prophecies from His birth to His accension that proved He is the Messiah.

Palace Dwellers know the truth. We have a relationship with Him. He is with us all the time. We can fellowship with Him. So, the Truth is in us. We are His. We have been set free by the power of His precious blood. Palace Dwellers are redeemed by the blood of the Lamb and filled with His Holy Spirit. We are forgiven and washed whiter than snow. We live with the knowledge of the truth that sets us free.

THE KINGDOM OF CREATIVITY

This Kingdom is the one we all must recognize is growing every day. From the arts, music, dance, design, painting, media, communications, performance sports—you name it—these areas continue to grow at a rapid pace. When it comes to creativity in the Kingdom, there is no end. The reason for this is simple. We were created to create. God created for six days and on the seventh day He rested. We too, create—whether it is a work we do with our minds or something we produce with our hands. There are those who create the great ideas, and those who bring those ideas into reality.

This Kingdom of Creativity has grown and will continue to grow because creating is a creative process that creates new ways to create new creations. The proof is all around us. Since the beginning of creation, all substances of the earth have been here. So, all we have created has been created from those God-given elements. We have new knowledge on how to combine and use these creations to create new things.

Metals have been synthesized from existing elements to make new metals that are stronger. Carbon fibers, plastics, and acrylics were all created from existing elements plus increased knowledge. Everything for a ship to fly to the moon existed in Noah's day. However, the knowledge and technology were not yet created.

It's plain to see that in many of the creative areas, man is trying to place his mark on creation. The earth, being a colony of Heaven, will always have the King's imprint. The King's imprint is all around us, we just must look. When we see how marvelous the human race is, we cannot help but see the Creator's design. When we see the geography of the earth and the other planets, we see His infinite majesty. When we see the ecosystems and how balanced and intricate they are, we can't help but see the King's imprint. Yes, we are created to create. Our goal in the palace life is to create that which will bring pleasure and glory to the King.

So, whatever you create, from a masterpiece painting to a wooden coffee table—do as unto the King. Create an atmosphere of praise and thanksgiving. Create an attitude of gratitude. Creating is what we do, creating an environment worthy of the King.

Kingdom of the Environment

The King reigns over all the earth. Home is where the heart is. As Palace Dwellers, we must know where our home really is. The scripture tells us we are sojourners. We are passing through. Heaven is our eternal home. That doesn't mean we pack our bags and sit by the door wanting to leave. We are to be living life abundantly here on earth until the King says we are done.

We are commanded in Genesis to dress, till and keep the earth. We are to take care of this beautiful gift the King has given to us. That doesn't mean that we let people die to save a tree or a spotted owl, but we must do whatever we can to take care of the earth. It's the only one we have for now. The physical environment is a grand display of the King's handiwork. But, if we don't dress, till and keep it, the earth will no longer reflect its King.

Recently, I had the privilege of seeing a movie called "Is Genesis History?" It is a must see. It examines Genesis from a scientific point of view. One of the best pieces of evidence for the history of Genesis is the Grand Canyon area. The scientists brought forth the two competing ideas. One was that there was a little water flowing through the rock over billions of years. The other (Biblical account) was that a lot of water flowed quickly cutting through rock like a water pressure cutting tool. They showed how the walls had very straight lines of differing color which indicates that this happened very quickly. I won't attempt to try to prove the Genesis flood. I don't have to. The King said it and that's good enough for me, but others may need more proof and while the King doesn't have to provide any, His planet will.

As we said earlier, creation can be seen all around us in every environment. Books upon books have and will be written displaying the King's majesty.

Our Home Should Reflect the King

When we speak of our home, we think of where we live. But what we should think is, where do our hearts and minds dwell? For example, someone moves to the United States from England, but everyday they still follow their European English customs of tea, etc. Their dwelling, the house where they sleep is in the United States, but their actions reflect their former homeland. While our house does take on a certain look, flavor, and style, the home in your heart is that place where you are you. No pretense, no mask, just the real you. It is where you feel the best, safest, and most comfortable.

Palace Dwellers feel best when in the King's presence. That's where we *should* feel the most comfortable—not afraid or uncomfortable but safe and secure. Where the spirit of the Lord is, there is freedom, joy, peace, and love. What an inviting home!

We like to personalize our homes with decorations and personal belongings, but the main thing our home environment should reflect is His presence.

We must also remember to not let our surroundings influence us as much as we influence our surroundings. In other words, create an environment conducive to Palace Living.

Kingdom of Time

God, our King, is eternal. He is the Alpha and Omega, the Beginning and the Ending. The Word tells us that a thousand years is as a day. Now, I don't believe that is an exact calculation as much as a general statement that time to God is all time. He sees all time, all the time. When we say God works in His timing, that means we may not see or live long enough to see how everything works out for His glory, His plan and His will.

We trust since He knows the beginning and the end, he also knows the in between; the here and now, the now and then, the past, the present and the future. The King sets the seasons not only of our physical environment, but of our very lives. We all go through seasons. These seasons are times of growth or new beginnings. Because we live in this world, we are hindered by its schedule. For example, I can't be in two places at the same time. We often try with technology to beat time restrictions by using video conferencing or livestreaming. But all of us have 24 hours in a day and at least 7 of those are needed for sleep! That leaves about 17 hours for work and play.

When we live in the Palace, the King does allow us freedom to spend that time the way we choose to, but I feel to be a good steward, we should follow Kingdom principles. Everything belongs to God thus all our time should be focused on the Kingdom. Seek first the Kingdom of God and His righteousness and all these things will be added unto you. Give yourself first to God and He (the Creator of all time) will bless you with all the time you need for all these things.

People are amazed at what can be accomplished when you give back the time God has given to you. People are also amazed that when they give God the money, energy, and talent that He has first given them—He multiplies it pressed down, shaken together and overflowing. It will never cease to amaze us how good God is.

The King's timing is always perfect. Never early, never late, always right on time. We must do our best to not waste time. Remember, time is the one thing that once you spend it, you can never get it back.

Here are some "time tested" sayings on time.

    Timing is everything

    It's about time

    Theres no time like the present

    Running out of time

    Time and time again

    Look how time flies

    Look at the time

    Old times

    Good times, bad times

    Time tested

    Time out

    Time of your life

    Exact time

    Great times

    Take time

    Make Time - The list goes on and on!!!

So, take time to pray. Take time to rest. Make time for relationships, especially with the King. There is never a better time than right now. Its time for life in the Palace.

KINGDOM OF THE SPIRIT REALM

Yes, our King is King of all. Many of us recognize the King as Ruler, however, He is ruler of every Kingdom whether we recognize it or not.

When Christ spoke, everyone listened. Some listened to try to catch Him in a misstatement. Some listened to learn, and others listened for entertainment. But, all who listened began to recognize that He spoke from a place of authority. Even those sent to spy on Him came back and reported that they had never heard anyone speak like this man (John 7:46). He spoke with authority because he was the Author, thus He spoke the truth.

When the King speaks, all hear and all come under His authority, even the spirit realm. Not just His followers, but even the enemy and legions of demons (Matthew 9:28-34). When Jesus spoke, the man possessed by legions of demons was freed as the demons came out. When He spoke to them, they recognized His authority and asked Him if He could send them into the herd of pigs. Some theologians believe this was better than being cast into the abyss. Life in a pig's body is better than no life. The owners of the pigs could not have been too happy when they ran off the edge of the cliff and perished.

Demons and Satan himself are subject to the King. Even though many people give them more power by allowing them to manifest, we need simply to say the Name of King (Jesus) and His authority must be obeyed. We have power, dominion and authority in His name. Unlike the movies that make the exorcism of demons a long hard process, I believe when we look to the King's example, we see that a word spoken with authority causes demons to tuck their tails and run. We are to flee temptation, not the devil. Submit yourselves then to God. Resist (fight) (stand) the devil and he will flee from you. (2 Timothy 2:22-24)

There are many tools the King gives us to fight, stand firm, or resist the devil and wickedness in the spirit realm.

>*Strive for holiness in the Word
>
>*Pray the Word
>
>*Do not doubt the power of the Holy Spirit
>
>*Mind your heart
>
>*Don't be proud
>
>*Keep the right attitude
>
>*Always resist using Jesus' authority and not your own.

Stand on the promises of God with strength and courage and Satan MUST flee. Remember, flee temptation quickly. Our King has authority in every Kingdom, including the spirit realm. Praise God!

CONCLUSION

We have moved from the pond to the Palace. We have seen through the eyes of His Word what Palace Living looks like. With all that has been given to us as Kingdom citizens, we should be forever rejoicing in the Lord. The Word tells us in Luke 17:21 that the Kingdom of God is manifest in Jesus the Messiah within you.

An invitation has been given to each of us, but we must accept, receive, and move into Palace Living. It is not only possible, but also probable that as we love, laugh, let go, let God, listen, learn and leap that we begin to live and see all that Palace Life has to offer.

Start your move to Palace Living today!

About the Author

Dr. David Donnally married the love of his life Tami, his high school sweetheart in 1978. She knelt beside him early 1977 as he was ordained into ministry, and so began their ministry life together. Although Dr. Donnally is the author of this book he acknowledges he could not have finished it without his wife. They are known as the dynamic duo as they have been serving God together through the good times and the bad.

Dr. Donnally holds a PhD in education, a PhD in Religious Education and a Doctorate in Theology. His ministry service included serving as Youth Pastor at the First Evangelical Lutheran Church in West Palm Beach, Youth pastor and Worship Leader at the Evangelical Bible Chapel, school teacher and school principal at Greenacres Christian Academy. (He and Tami co-founded Greenacres Christian Academy in 1980 along with his parents, Drs. Chadwick and Mariam Donnally)

He currently serves as Executive Pastor and President of Legacy Church Ministries, President (and Professor) of the Evangelical Bible College and Seminary.

He also is founder of the Interdenominational Ministers

Association and the House of Bread, (both founded in 2003), and Compassionate Heart Counseling Center founded in 2014.

He serves on many different ministry boards and offers his many years of experience to help them navigate ministry life. He is known as husband, Dad, Grandpa, (the man, the myth, the legend) by his family, Pastor Dave by all of his past students in the school, Pastor Donnally by his parishioners, Dr. Donnally by his college students and friend by many. But most of all a child of the King of kings and Lord of lords. Pouring into others the knowledge of the Kingdom of God to further God's influence in this culture for His glory has been his life passion.

His first book "From the Pond to the Palace" was a look at his life and the seven hops or moves that enables one to move closer to Palace Living.

This book (Life in the Palace) takes a deeper look into what our lives should look like when we are citizens of the King & filled with His Spirit.

Dr. Donnally's deepest desire is for all who read these books to be inspired to start living the Kingdom life now and influencing those around us with The Good News and Kingdom life.

www.ingramcontent.com/pod-product-compliance
Lightning Source LLC
Chambersburg PA
CBHW050744170426
43193CB00033BA/1657